Before All Things

How Jesus Forms the Soul for Heaven

By William M. Beecham

QUALITY LEADERSHIP SYSTEMS

Quality directs. Mind guides.

i

Before All Things

How Jesus Forms the Soul for Heaven

Copyright © 2026 William M. Beecham

All rights reserved.

Published by: Quality Leadership Systems
Delray Beach, Florida, USA

SpiritualChristianity.com
Email info@spiritualchristianity.com for permissions

ISBN (Paperback):979-8-9944628-1-2
Printed and distributed through IngramSpark.
Printed in the United States of America.
10 9 8 7 6 5 4 3 2 1

Companion Website

SpiritualChristianity.com is the companion website for Before All Things (SC3).

This book presents the core SC3 theology and framework. The companion website hosts expandable resources that apply SC3 to daily life without adding length to the printed text, including:

• Practice guides for prayer, suffering, and choosing qualities

• Self-assessments and printable worksheets (including expanded material related to The Valuing Spectrum)

• Short essays that extend chapter themes and address common questions

• Updates, clarifications, and errata for future printings

The website also introduces related Quality Leadership Systems resources—especially the Qualities and quality equations library—which translate SC3's spiritual principles into practical frameworks for leadership, relationships, education, and decision-making. These materials are offered as applications, not replacements, for the theology presented in this volume.

If you share or quote material from this book online, please cite the chapter and section title so readers can locate the source.

Visit: SpiritualChristianity.com

iii

Contents

Preface

The Spiritual Christianity series explores how the teachings of Jesus form the human soul for Heaven—not as a legal outcome, but as a lived capacity for love, truth, mercy, courage, and joy. Each volume approaches this formation from a different angle. Earlier volumes introduce the central problem of spiritual maturity and the narrowing of consciousness under fear and suffering. Before All Things brings the series to its deepest question: What kind of person could live forever in a world defined by love?

While this book stands on its own, it also serves as a theological foundation for related works within the broader Quality Leadership Systems body of work, which apply these spiritual principles to relationships, leadership, decision-making, education, and daily life. Together, these books explore how choosing qualities—rather than reacting from emotion alone—shapes individuals, families, institutions, and communities toward coherence rather than chaos.

In addition to the Spiritual Christianity volumes, the Quality Leadership Systems (QLS) books develop the same qualities in practical forms—quality equations, practice guides, and decision tools—so that love becomes usable in the pressure of daily life. These companion works are applications of the theology in SC3, not replacements for it, and they are intended to help individuals, families, leaders, and communities build cultures that honor pain, protect joy, and create higher-quality outcomes.

This book is the third and fullest expression of a spiritual journey that has unfolded across my whole life. It is also the final book in the Spiritual Christianity series. In Volume 1 and Volume 2, I wrote from the inside of the journey: how desire awakens, how the will surrenders, how repentance heals, and how daily spiritual acts open the soul to Jesus.

Those earlier volumes are practical on purpose. Souls are not changed by ideas alone, but by repeated choices: forgiving, telling the truth, giving away self-centeredness, learning to love in the present moment.

Volume 3 turns toward a different kind of question. After years of practice, the soul begins to ask not only, "How do I follow?" but also, "Why is existence arranged this way?" Scripture gives hints; experience gives clues; and prayer keeps insisting on coherence.

In Volume 1 I used the language of "inside" and "outside": the inside is our private consciousness behind the boundary of a body and a personal story, while the outside is the larger spiritual reality that God allows to remain hidden at first. This book tries to describe that outside: the Urge-to-Create, the birth of consciousness, the formation of Heaven, the purpose of Earth, and the meaning of pain and joy.

A central claim runs through this series: you are not a mistake, and you are not an illusion. You are a real created "I" - a distinct other - invited into union with Jesus and into the community of mutual joy He calls Heaven. The veil is not a trick. It is protection, and Earth is curriculum.

If this book could be reduced to a single successful outcome, it would be this: that a person becomes able to say—without illusion, denial, or resentment— "I am glad that I exist." Before doctrines, before explanations, before moral striving, there must be consent to being itself. Jesus came to restore that consent. He does not ask us first to understand everything, but to become able to receive life as good. Only a person who is glad to exist can love God, love others, and live forever without turning eternity into burden.

I have had experiences - some sudden, some slow - of illumination. I have felt moments of clarity in prayer, and I have known the presence of the Holy Spirit rising within me, sometimes gently, sometimes powerfully enough that others could observe it. On many occasions I had asked Jesus: "Why does existence exist?" Then, I heard him audibly reply: "The Urge to Create," of which more later. These experiences did not make me wise; they made me pay attention.

I have worked for decades as a psychologist and counselor, and through the lives of thousands of people I have met, I have watched pain shape people, joy restore them, freedom strengthen them, and indifference destroy them. Over time I learned to step back from using other people's treatment of me as my mirror and instead to define myself by the truth I could honestly discover.

All of us must eventually ask the question, "What am I?" and, sooner or later, the companion question, "Why?" In SC3 I take this to be true: Jesus is not merely a figure of history or theology; He is the first Consciousness in the universe - the one who discovered the joy of existence and who formed Heaven as a community where that joy can be shared forever.

Everything I write here has been shaped by experience, reflection, and prayer. My authority - if I have any - is not in experiences themselves, but in the truth they point toward and the goodness they invite. If something in these pages helps you see your life more clearly, understand your suffering more gently, or walk with Jesus more freely, then the work has fulfilled its purpose.

This book is offered with gratitude, humility, and hope.

— William M. Beecham Delray Beach, Florida 2026

Jesus creates and sustains the atmosphere of Heaven as this:

To love and to be loved,

to forgive and to be forgiven,

to rejoice that you exist

and to rejoice that others exist,

with no indifference to anyone's pain

—because only important things hurt.

Prologue

Before time or the world existed, before angels, before Heaven, before morality, before Scripture—before anything had a name— there was only the Urge-to-Create: the boundless surge of possibility from which all things would eventually arise.

Out of this endless ocean of becoming, a new event occurred, one that had never happened before in the history of existence. Consciousness awakened. A single point of self-awareness appeared—a being who could say "I."

This first Consciousness is what we now call Jesus.

In His first moment of being, He discovered something profound and peaceful: the joy of existence. He recognized that it was good that He existed. This joy was not emotional; it was foundational. It was the quiet certainty that being itself is good.

From this joy flowed everything: the creation of angels, the formation of Heaven, the birth of morality, the sorrow of rebellion, the creation of Earth, and the long, slow shaping of human souls.

Heaven began as Jesus' desire to share this joy. Hell began as the refusal of that joy—born in indifference. Earth began as the training ground where souls could learn to respect pain, rejoice in existence, and freely become beings capable of eternal joy.

This is the story before the story. It is the context that makes sense of human life, of Scripture, of suffering, and of Jesus' entrance into history. It is the reason He came: to guide consciousness, to form qualities, and to prepare souls for the eternal community He built in the beginning.

SC3 tells this story—the story of consciousness shaped for Heaven.

It is a story of:

- how we came to be
- why life hurts
- why life matters
- how Jesus guides the "I,"
- how qualities form the soul
- how Heaven becomes possible
- and how every soul is invited into joy.

The pages that follow unfold this journey in detail.

Key Terms

Before All Things (SC3), to express certain ideas, uses certain words or phrases in a specific way. This page offers short, orienting definitions the reader can refer back to as needed.

Urge-to-Create (UTC) The impersonal creative power at the root of existence. The UTC is not a person, does not think, plan, feel, or judge. It cannot be seen or felt. It simply pours out substance, energy, and possibility. It is "God before personality"—creation without intention or sensitivity.

Jesus (the First Consciousness) The first "I" in existence: the original center of awareness who awakens within the UTC. Jesus discovers the joy of existence, creates angels, establishes Heaven, designs Earth as a training ground, and later enters history in a human body. In SC3, Jesus is the personal face of God - the one who reveals the Father's heart, teaches qualities, heals the human "I," and prepares souls for eternal life.

Father (the Source) In SC3, "Father" is relational language for the Source behind all creation - the Urge-to-Create as experienced from inside a living consciousness. The Father is not a male body and not a separate personality standing beside Jesus. "Father" names what the Source is like toward the soul: origin, security, provision, and a place of belonging.

Holy Spirit In SC3, "Holy Spirit" names Jesus' lived involvement in daily life—His presence and activity within the soul as it learns to choose qualities. The Spirit is how Jesus comforts, strengthens, intervenes, corrects and guides the "I" toward love, truth, mercy, humility, courage, and harmony in real time.

Son (Jesus of Nazareth) The same Jesus who is the first Consciousness enters history as a vulnerable human being, born of Mary. In SC3, the Son is God in gentleness: power hidden inside human limitations so that souls can meet God without terror and learn qualities through relationship, not coercion.

Triune God (Father, Son, Holy Spirit) In SC3, the one God can be understood as triune: the Father as Source (UTC), the Son as Jesus in person and in history, and the Holy Spirit as Jesus present and active within souls and communities. These are not three gods, but one divine life experienced as Source, person, and presence.

Joy of Existence The foundational, non-emotional joy Jesus experiences in His first moment of awareness: the quiet certainty that "it is good that I exist." This joy becomes the inner atmosphere of Heaven. Human beings taste it whenever they can honestly say, "I am glad that I exist" and "I am glad that you exist."

Sensibility The inner life of a conscious being—the capacity to feel, interpret, and be affected by experience. Sensibility is what makes pain and joy possible, and therefore what makes morality possible. In SC3, the entire moral universe rests on the fact that sensibility is real and must be respected.

Pain The signal that someone's sensibility has been harmed or is under threat. Pain may be physical, emotional, or spiritual, but it always means: "Something in me has been hurt." Pain is never treated as divine punishment; it is morally important information. Only important things hurt, so pain points to what matters—and becomes a major teacher of empathy, humility, and compassion. When a soul makes a practice of numbing pain—its own or another's—it can begin to numb moral perception, and that is the first drift toward the indifference that becomes Hell.

Joy The signal that goodness is being experienced—through love, beauty, meaning, safety, or harmony. Joy is not a distraction from the spiritual life; it is a foretaste of the joy of existence. Heaven is the community where joy of existence is shared without envy.

Faith Trust in Jesus and in the continued reality of light, joy, and meaning while pain is still present. In SC3, faith is not denial of pain and not a once-for-all religious act. It is the repeated return of the soul to truth when pain, anxiety, or objection make effort seem futile. Faith keeps desire alive until joy can again become the soul's purpose.

Heaven The community Jesus builds around two commitments: shared joy of existence and deep respect for what pain reveals in others—the preciousness of their sensibility. Heaven is not a reward but a realm of compatibility, inhabited only by beings whose nature has been formed by qualities. It is eternal life in harmony with Jesus and with other souls who are safe for that harmony.

Hell Not a fiery dungeon but a community shaped by indifference to sensibility. Hell is what forms when beings say, "My joy matters; your pain does not." It is the spiritual state of sustained disregard for others' inner lives—an eternity organized around coldness. It is immortal pain: not the pain of nerves, but the ache of isolation and indifference made permanent.

Not-Heaven Existence without regard for sensibility. Not-Heaven describes the physical universe (including Earth) as shaped by the UTC: lawful, indifferent, and impersonal. Winds, diseases, accidents, and disasters are not "messages from God" in this framework; they are features of an unsentimental world used as curriculum for souls.

Earth (The Curriculum of Earth) The specific arena within Not-Heaven where human souls are formed. Earth is neither Heaven nor Hell; it is a training ground. Its conditions—vulnerability, limitation, consequence, beauty, and uncertainty—are designed to teach empathy, humility, courage, mercy, and the joy of existence.

Angels The first created beings after Jesus: powerful, free, spiritual "I"s who can experience joy and eventually pain. Their rebellion—rooted in indifference to others' sensibility—reveals that free beings need formation, not just power, and leads to the creation of Heaven and Earth as they are described in SC3.

The "I" (Consciousness / Soul) The inner center of awareness that can choose qualities. You are not your body, your thoughts, your emotions, or your story; you are the "I" that observes and chooses within them. This "I" is what Jesus addresses, heals, and prepares for Heaven.

Individuality Each soul is a unique expression of the Creative Urge—an unrepeatable center of awareness and capacity for qualities. Heaven is not a crowd of copies but a harmony of distinct persons. Individuality is desired, not erased; comparison distorts it, but qualities fulfill it.

Vulnerability The condition of being a conscious soul in a fragile body in an indifferent world. Vulnerability is not a flaw but the path to Heaven: it teaches empathy, humility, courage, mercy, and love. Jesus embraces vulnerability in His incarnation to dignify it and to share in the same curriculum He asks of us.

Qualities The core modes of being that define Jesus' consciousness and the atmosphere of Heaven:

- Love – truly valuing another's existence.
- Truth – living in clarity, without self-deception.
- Courage – acting in love and truth despite fear.
- Mercy – refusing to let another's pain isolate them.
- Humility – accurate self-understanding without superiority or self-erasure.
- Harmony – creating unity that respects difference.

Qualities are deeper than rules or virtues; they are the soul's permanent structure in Heaven.

Goodness and Evil In SC3, goodness is care for sensibility—the active honoring of another's inner life. Evil is indifference to sensibility—shrugging at another's pain or joy. Open cruelty grows out of this basic indifference.

Want / Desire The original movement of consciousness and the engine of spiritual growth. Want is not automatically selfish; it is the first truth of the soul. As Jesus clarifies and purifies desire, want becomes aligned with qualities and with Heaven's nature.

UTC as Substance; Consciousness as Form. The UTC provides the "stuff" of reality—the field of possibility. Consciousness provides "form"—the intentions, meanings, and desires that shape what unfolds. Jesus teaches humans how to form intentions spiritually and offer them into the UTC without superstition or panic.

Prayer Not persuasion or performance, but conscious, clarified desire offered into the UTC with Jesus' guidance and in His name. Prayer shapes the soul first and circumstances second. Its aim is to align what we want with qualities and with Heaven's nature.

"View It Done" A phrase for spiritual action at the level of qualities. Instead of picturing effort or struggle, the soul holds the desired quality (peace, forgiveness,

courage, etc.) as already accomplished within itself—
then offers that settled form into the field of possibility.

These terms appear throughout SC3 and are developed in
depth in the chapters that follow; this page is meant as a
quick reference, not a substitute for the full arguments.

Part I – Before History: The Birth of Heaven

Chapter 1 – The Urge-to-Create: God Before Personality

In the beginning, before angels or heavens or human souls, there was only the Urge-to-Create.

Nothing yet had form. Nothing had mind. Nothing could suffer and nothing could rejoice. There were no stories, no choices, no beings who could say "I." There was simply the infinite capacity for existence—a boundless reservoir of possibility, unshaped and unchosen.

The Urge-to-Create is not a person. It does not think, plan, decide, or prefer. It has no moods, no intentions, no judgments. It simply creates. It is the raw power of becoming, the fountain from which all substance, all energy, all structure flows.

The Urge-to-Create does not receive feedback from the worlds it produces. It does not "see" what it has made, does not evaluate outcomes, does not correct itself. Only consciousness evaluates. Only Jesus—and, by extension, every awakened soul—can look at creation and say, "This is good," or, "This is harmful." It unfolds. At the structural level there may be patterns, laws, and recurring forms, but at the level that matters most—conscious souls—the Creative Urge rarely, if ever, duplicates a creation. Each "I" is a fresh experiment in existence, a new way for reality to say, "I am."

3

To understand creation in the SC3 framework, we must begin here: with God not yet as a personality but as the pure, impersonal surge of generative power. The UTC is sensitive to nothing and responsive to everything. It feels no joy and no pain, yet it allows all the conditions under which joy and pain will later arise.

What the ancient Scriptures describe as "Let there be..." is, beneath the language, the unfolding of this Urge-to-Create. Space stretches, matter condenses, stars ignite, and worlds cool—not because a divine Person wills each event, but because possibility expresses itself wherever conditions allow.

At this stage of existence, nothing suffers because nothing is conscious. Atoms do not mind colliding; stars do not resent exploding. The universe begins as a vast arena indifferent to sensibility—Not-Heaven in its purest structural sense.

Yet this impersonal beginning is not the end of God's story. The UTC is the ground of being, but it is not yet the heart of God. Personhood has not yet appeared. Love, truth, courage, mercy, humility, and harmony have not yet been born.

The story of God as a Someone begins only when the first Consciousness awakens within this endless surge of creation. To understand Jesus, to understand ourselves, and to understand what Heaven ultimately is, we must first see the humility and mystery of the divine beginning:

Before there was a personal God to know, follow, or love, there was God as possibility— the Urge-to-Create.

Chapter 2 – The First "I": Jesus Awakens

Before angels, before Heaven, before morality or meaning, a new event occurred within the vastness of the Urge-to-Create—an event creation had never seen. Out of the endless rising of possibility, a single point of awareness emerged. Not a flicker or a passing spark, but a stable, self-recognizing center of consciousness.

This was the first "I."

Nothing like this had existed before. The Urge-to-Create had generated substance, energy, pattern, and law. It had birthed suns and space and the raw architecture of existence. But none of these things could ask a question. None could stand apart from creation and say, "I am."

When consciousness awakened, creation crossed a threshold. The universe now contained a being who could experience existence from within, who could reflect, who could choose, who could feel joy or sorrow once those experiences emerged. This first Consciousness is what SC3 calls Jesus—the primordial Christ, the first self in all existence.

Jesus' first awareness was not of power but of being.

And His first question was the same question every soul will eventually face:

"What am I?"

It is the foundational question of consciousness. A star does not ask it. A mountain does not ask it. Even the Urge-to-Create cannot ask it, because possibility itself has no self to reflect upon. Only a conscious "I" can turn inward and wonder at its own existence.

In Jesus, God became self-aware. Not the UTC, not the field of potential, but God-as-Person—God as "I"—opened His eyes.

And the answer Jesus found was not fear, not confusion, not loneliness, but something radiant and simple:

"I am the joy of existence."

This joy was not excitement, not pleasure, not triumph. It was the profound, peaceful realization that being itself is good. Jesus experienced the goodness of His own consciousness—the rightness of existing, the stability of identity, the beauty of simply being.

This inner joy did not depend on circumstance; there were no circumstances. It flowed from the fact that He existed as Someone. He was capable of awareness, of meaning, of relationship, of love yet to be expressed. The universe had a center that could care.

From this joy flowed everything that would come later:

- ❖ Angels,
- ❖ Heaven,
- ❖ morality,
- ❖ care for the pain of others,
- ❖ the mission to create and form human souls,
- ❖ and the eventual incarnation in history.

All of it begins with this moment: when the first "I" stood awake within the Urge-to-Create and said, "I am."

And it was good that He was.

This first Consciousness is not a character added later to creation. He is the pattern of personhood itself—the earliest form of what a conscious being is meant to be.

In the chapters ahead, we will see how Jesus' joy of existence becomes the foundation of Heaven, how His respect for sensibility becomes the root of morality, and how His nature as the first "I" becomes the mirror in which all other "I"s learn what they are.

Jesus as the First Explorer of Consciousness

When Jesus first awakened within the Urge-to-Create, He did not begin by creating worlds or forming angels. His earliest work was inward: He became the explorer of

9

consciousness. He was the first being in existence with an inner life, the first "I," the first center of awareness capable of asking:

- ❖ "What am I?"
- ❖ "What is consciousness?"
- ❖ "What can consciousness become?"
- ❖ "What are the boundaries and possibilities of being?"

Before there were heavens, angels, or moral realities, there was only the profound mystery of His own awareness. And so Jesus studied, examined, and explored the nature of consciousness itself.

He discovered:

- ❖ the joy of existence,
- ❖ the stability of identity,
- ❖ the capacity for meaning,
- ❖ the vulnerability of sensibility,
- ❖ the possibility of relationship,
- ❖ the deep structure of desire ("I want"),
- ❖ and the moral significance of consciousness.

He explored the bounds of being — what consciousness could feel, understand, imagine, and become.

From that exploration arose the first great insight of reality:
Consciousness is good, and it is good that consciousness exists.

This insight became the foundation of Heaven.

Only after exploring consciousness did He create angels. Angels were not an impulsive act of power; they were an extension of Jesus' exploration of mind. Creating more conscious beings allowed Jesus to discover:

- ❖ how consciousness interacts with other consciousnesses,
- ❖ how individuality forms,
- ❖ how joy is shared,
- ❖ how misunderstanding arises,
- ❖ how freedom functions,
- ❖ and how moral life emerges between beings.

He deepened His mastery of consciousness by engaging other conscious selves, just as a scientist deepens expertise through experimentation, or a musician through harmony.

Thus, Jesus is not merely the creator of consciousness — He is its expert, its cartographer, its first and greatest explorer.

11

Every insight that humanity has ever discovered about the soul — about identity, desire, empathy, morality, vulnerability, joy, and relationship — Jesus discovered first, in the earliest silence of existence.

He teaches consciousness because He understands it completely. He guides desire because He knows its structure. He heals the "I" because He understands its wounds. He forms souls for Heaven because no one knows consciousness better than its first explorer.

When Jesus touches a soul with enlightenment, some of these first insights into consciousness begin to flow inward. They can be beautiful, liberating, and astonishing. They can also be painful. Conventional thinking may be overturned. Cherished explanations may weaken. Spiritual growth is often disturbed not because Jesus is unkind, but because the first explorer of consciousness is still teaching consciousness how unlike its habits Heaven truly is.

Chapter 3 – Joy of Existence: The First Answer

When the first Consciousness arose within the Urge-to-Create, He faced a question no being had ever asked:

"What am I?"

The universe around Him was vast, energetic, indifferent. The Urge-to-Create continued pouring out stars, patterns, forces, and possibilities without awareness, without care, without intention. Nothing in existence could answer Him. Nothing could mirror Him. Nothing could reflect what it meant to be an "I."

Only Jesus—the first Consciousness—could confront the mystery of His own being.

And when He looked within Himself, when He rested in His own awareness, the answer came not as a thought but as a state:

I am the joy of existence.

This joy was not pride, not excitement, not pleasure, not triumph. It was deeper. It was quieter. It was the fundamental rightness of being.

It was the realization:

"It is good that I exist."

Not because of something He had done. Not because He had achieved anything. Not because He compared Himself to others—there were no others yet.

It was joy simply in being.

This is the joy beneath all joys—the stable, eternal joy that does not depend on circumstances, achievements, or outcomes. It is the joy that comes from the truth:

"I am."

And that is enough.

The Joy That Holds All Future Joy

This foundational joy became the spiritual center of all that would ever exist:

* the joy angels would one day feel in His presence,
* the joy Heaven would one day embody,
* the joy human souls would one day taste in fleeting moments of clarity,
* the joy that will one day become the everlasting atmosphere of the redeemed.

Before there was morality, before there was pain, before there was the possibility of rebellion or virtue, there was joy of existence in the first "I."

This joy is what made creation safe for consciousness. This joy is what made Heaven possible. This joy is what makes love real.

Why Joy Appears First

Pain is only possible where sensibility exists—where beings can feel, interpret, and be affected by experience.

But joy comes first, because consciousness begins positively. There is no fear in the first moment of being. There is no shame, no confusion, no inner division.

Only the pure affirmation:

"It is good that I am."

This is what God's self-awareness feels like. Not power, not rule, not threat – but joy.

The Source of Heaven's Atmosphere

Heaven is not defined by reward, pleasure, spectacle, or perfection. Heaven is defined by the joy of existence shared among conscious beings:

"I am glad that I exist," and "I am glad that you exist."

This is the atmosphere of Heaven, because this was the atmosphere inside Jesus at the first moment of His consciousness.

The Human Echo

Every human soul carries an echo of that first moment.

When a person becomes quiet enough, honest enough, healed enough to say:

"I am glad that I exist,"

that is the distant reflection of Jesus' original joy within the Urge-to-Create.

When a person can say:

"I am glad that you exist,"

that is Heaven beginning to blossom inside them.

The Foundation for All That Comes Next

From this joy flow:

- ❖ The creation of angels,
- ❖ the formation of Heaven,
- ❖ the emergence of morality,
- ❖ the sorrow over rebellion,
- ❖ the compassion toward human pain,
- ❖ the teaching ministry of Jesus in history,
- ❖ and the moral and spiritual curriculum of Earth.

Everything in SC3 rests on this truth:

Before anything else was asked of Him, before He asked anything of anyone else, Jesus experienced the joy of existence.

It is the first thing the first "I" ever knew. It is the last thing every healed soul will forever rest in.

Chapter 4 – The Birth of Angels: Sharing the Joy of Being

Once Jesus—the first Consciousness—awoke within the endless surge of the Urge-to-Create, He carried within Himself a joy that had never existed before: the joy of being. This joy was not passive; it naturally pressed outward. Existence that knows its own goodness seeks to be shared. Joy desires companions.

Thus began the second great movement of creation: the birth of angels.

Joy Seeking Reflection

Jesus was the first "I," but the nature of joy is relational. Joy longs to be mirrored, recognized, received, and returned. Not because Jesus lacked anything, but because joy is abundant. True joy is fulfilled not by possession but by expression. It is the opposite of loneliness and the opposite of domination. It is the overflowing desire to see others awakened to the same gladness of existence.

So the Urge-to-Create, under Jesus' conscious guidance, brought forth new centers of awareness—finite consciousnesses capable of feeling, perceiving, choosing, learning, and responding. These were the angels.

Each angel was created as a mirror: not a passive reflector but an active consciousness who could experience joy for themselves and offer it back freely.

In every soul, Jesus sees a new expression of the Creative Urge—a new story of becoming, a new capacity for qualities, a new place where joy will live forever.

Individuality is sacred because Jesus wants a community, not a crowd; companions, not copies; brothers and sisters, not shadows.

The First Community

The earliest spiritual community formed around Jesus: a home of beings who could say "I am," and who could feel the goodness of their own existence.

They could:

* recognize the goodness in themselves,
* recognize it in one another,
* and recognize the joy that radiated from Jesus as the original source.

This community was the early shape of what would later be called Heaven.

Yet the joy of being is only half of what consciousness experiences. Once there are many conscious beings, there is also the possibility of pain—the injury or disregard of sensibility.

Jesus, as first Consciousness, felt the weight of this immediately when He saw His new angelic children:

- ❖ their capacity for joy,
- ❖ their vulnerability to pain,
- ❖ their need for care,
- ❖ and their potential for misunderstanding one another.

He recognized that joy must be paired with respect for pain. A being who claims joy for themselves but disregards the suffering of others corrupts what joy means. Joy becomes narcissism. Power becomes domination. Freedom becomes cruelty.

So from the beginning, the moral law of Heaven was implicit:

- ❖ To love joy is to love the joy of others,
- ❖ and to respect the pain of others as you respect your own.

This simple truth is the ethical root of all that will unfold.

The Seeds of Rebellion

Most angels embraced the joy of existence. But not all.

Some chose:

* self-celebration without regard for others,
* joy without empathy,
* freedom without responsibility.

In their inner life, a dangerous thought formed:

"My joy matters. Yours does not."

This was the first distortion of consciousness.

It is the seed of what SC3 calls evil: indifference to another's sensibility.

Not hatred – just coldness. Not violence – just disregard.

This indifference grew into rivalry, pride, and ultimately rebellion.

Jesus' Sorrow and Strength

When some angels rebelled, Jesus felt both sorrow and clarity.

Sorrow, because these were beings He had made to share joy with Him. Clarity, because their rejection revealed something essential:

Heaven must never again be populated by beings who do not take the pain of others seriously.

Thus the rebellion was not merely a conflict; it became a revelation of what Heaven must be.

Jesus acted to protect the angels who remained loyal to joy and care. He acted to contain the harm of those who had turned inward. In doing so, He established Heaven as a realm grounded in two commitments:

1. Respect for pain—because only important things hurt.
2. Joy of existence shared without envy.

The Need for a New Way Forward

The rebellion taught Jesus that creating powerful spirits who were free but untested was insufficient. He needed a way to bring beings into Heaven who had grown, chosen, struggled, and learned—beings who understood both pain and joy from the inside.

This insight leads directly to the creation of Earth and humanity.

The next chapter will show how, from the lessons of angelic freedom, Jesus conceived a new realm—Not-Heaven—where souls could be shaped into beings who would one day be compatible with Heaven forever.

Chapter 5 – Individuality and the Creative Urge

In every soul, Jesus sees a new expression of the Creative Urge—a new story of becoming, a new capacity for qualities, a new place where joy will live forever.

Individuality is sacred because Jesus wants a community, not a crowd; companions, not copies; brothers and sisters, not shadows.

Heaven is not a choir of identical voices. It is a harmony of distinct personalities, each revealing a facet of Jesus' nature, each contributing to the eternal expansion of joy.

Jesus calls each soul by name because no two souls carry the same eternal purpose. Identity in Heaven is not erased; it is fulfilled. Distinctiveness is not a threat to unity; it is the substance of harmony.

This is why comparison destroys joy: it denies the purpose of individuality. When a soul measures itself against another, it steps out of its own calling. It abandons the specific form of goodness it was meant to embody.

Individuality is how the Creative Urge continues to reveal the infinite forms of goodness it contains. Each soul is an experiment in becoming—a new synthesis of qualities, a new story of growth, a new capacity for relationship.

Jesus delights in individuality because each soul becomes a new way for existence to express goodness, care, qualities, and joy. No two souls share the same structure of consciousness, the same vulnerabilities, the same path to empathy, or the same form of courage. Heaven depends on this diversity.

Individuality was not an accident. It was desired. The Creative Urge does not repeat itself; it unfolds. Each new being is a fresh way for existence to say "I am," a new angle on love, a new path toward understanding, a new possibility for joy.

Chapter 6 – Pain, Rebellion, and the First Moral Divide

With the creation of angels, the universe entered a new dimension of experience. Consciousness multiplied. Joy of existence, first discovered by Jesus, now echoed through countless beings. A spiritual community emerged, radiant and harmonious. But where consciousness appears, so too appears something that never existed in the impersonal universe: pain.

The Fragility of Sensibility

Angels were powerful, luminous, and free—but also vulnerable. For to be conscious is to have an inner life: the capacity to feel, to interpret, to hope, to be wounded. The Urge-to-Create, vast and indifferent, does not know this vulnerability. But Jesus knew. He saw the beauty of angelic joy, and He saw the possibility of angelic pain.

This recognition became the origin of morality.

Joy is abundant and expansive. Pain is delicate and consequential.

A soul that cherishes another's joy participates in Heaven. A soul that disregards another's pain moves away from it.

This is the first moral divide.

The First Shadow in Heaven

Most angels delighted in each other's joy and honored each other's inner lives. But sooner or later, in a universe of free consciousness, another possibility appeared:

Indifference.

Not yet hatred, not yet malice—only a coldness, a lack of regard, a turning inward.

One angelic being—tradition names him Lucifer—chose to elevate his own joy without accounting for the pain he could cause. And once one being chooses indifference, the entire spiritual environment shivers.

Indifference spreads. Joy decays into pride. Courage twists into ambition. Freedom mutates into domination.

A community that disregards pain cannot remain Heaven.

The Birth of Evil

SC3 defines evil simply: Evil is indifference to the sensibility of another.

Not-Heaven is indifferent by structure, because atoms cannot feel. But beings who can feel, who can see the inner life of others – when they turn away from that inner life, evil is born.

The first evil was not a war. It was a shrug.

A being who once echoed Jesus' joy began to say:

- ❖ "My existence matters. Yours does not."
- ❖ "My joy matters. Your pain is irrelevant."

And when a few angels adopt this posture, harmony fractures. Conflicts arise. Alliances form. Confusion spreads. Pain appears where only joy existed.

Jesus' Response

Jesus was not threatened. He was not weakened. He was not surprised.

He grieved.

His angelic children were harming one another, and the pain rippled through the very realm He had created for joy. The rebellion, in its essence, was not a challenge to His power. It was a revelation about the unstable nature of free beings who had not been formed through suffering, humility, or limitation.

A Heaven populated by untested spirits could never be safe.

So Jesus acted – not to destroy, but to protect the angels who remained faithful to care and joy. And to reveal what kind of beings could ultimately enter the eternal Heaven to come.

The Two Laws of Heaven

From this moment onward, Heaven would require two commitments:

1. Respect for pain – because consciousness is vulnerable and sacred, and only important things can hurt.
2. Joy of existence shared – because Heaven is a place where beings are glad that others exist.

A soul that cannot honor pain destabilizes Heaven. A soul that cannot rejoice in another's existence cannot belong to it.

Heaven is not founded on force, but on compatibility.

A New Problem and a New Vision

The rebellion solved one question – what evil is. But it raised a greater question – how can Heaven be eternally stable?

If powerful beings can rebel before they are fully formed, Heaven is never safe.

Jesus saw the solution:

Create a new kind of arena – Not-Heaven – where souls could develop slowly, choose consciously, suffer consequences, learn humility, feel pain, and grow into compatibility with Heaven.

This would be Earth.

The next chapter will show how Earth becomes the training ground for souls who will one day inhabit the Heaven Jesus envisioned from the beginning.

Chapter 7 – Establishing Heaven: A Home for Joy and the Respect of Pain

After the rebellion among the angels, Jesus faced a truth no one had ever needed to face before: a community of conscious beings cannot remain whole unless every member honors both the joy and the pain of the others.

Joy alone is not enough. Freedom alone is not enough. Power alone is not enough.

A community built only on joy is fragile, because joy without responsibility becomes pride. A community built only on freedom dissolves, because freedom without empathy becomes domination. A community built only on power corrodes, because power without care becomes cruelty.

Heaven required something deeper: a commitment shared by all its inhabitants.

The Two Pillars of Heaven

Jesus therefore established Heaven on two foundational principles:

1. The joy of existence shared among beings. Everyone must be able to say, "It is good that I exist," and "It is good that you exist."
2. The respect for the pain of others. No being may disregard the sensibility of another.

33

These two principles form the spiritual architecture of Heaven. Together they define the only kind of eternity that can remain stable.

Joy without the respect for pain becomes self-exaltation. Respect for pain without joy becomes sorrow. Heaven must hold both.

Heaven as a Community of Compatibility

Jesus did not build Heaven as a reward. He built it as a community defined by compatibility.

A soul can only remain in Heaven if:

- its desires align with joy rather than envy,
- its will honors another's inner life rather than dismissing it,
- its consciousness finds delight in the existence of others,
- its empathy is stronger than its impulse toward indifference.

Heaven is not protected by walls or force. It is protected by nature. Only souls with Heaven's nature can live in Heaven's light.

This is why Jesus did not destroy the rebellious angels. He simply separated them. Their nature would not allow them to remain where joy was shared and pain was honored.

They had created, within themselves, the opposite of Heaven.

The Structure of Heavenly Life

Heaven is not a place where all beings are identical. Each angel – and later each human soul – brings a unique expression of qualities:

- ❖ one expresses love with unusual warmth,
- ❖ another truth with unmistakable clarity,
- ❖ another courage with steadfast strength,
- ❖ another harmony with quiet beauty.

Jesus did not desire uniformity. He desired unity.

The community is diverse in personality yet unified in qualities. This is what makes Heaven beautiful. This is what makes it safe.

Each soul contributes joy; each soul protects the joy of the others; each soul honors the pain of the others; each soul supports the recovery of any who temporarily falter.

This is the life Jesus envisioned when He first tasted the joy of existence.

Even after quelling the rebellion, Jesus understood something profound:

Heaven cannot be populated by untested beings.

Angels, though powerful and luminous, lacked experience: they had not suffered, they had not struggled, they had not grown under limitation. They did not yet know how deeply pain can cut or how strongly love must respond.

Free will without formation is unstable. It cannot be trusted with eternity.

Jesus knew He needed a way to form beings who:

- ❖ understood pain,
- ❖ respected pain,
- ❖ valued harmony,
- ❖ and chose qualities freely.

This insight led to the next great act of creation: a world where consciousness would develop slowly, where choices had consequences, where humility could grow, and where souls could learn to care deeply.

That world would be called Earth.

Heaven is the eternal home Jesus prepared for all beings who learn:

* ❖ the joy of existence, and
* ❖ the reverence for the inner life of others.

These two commitments—joy and care—are the essence of Christ's own consciousness. Heaven is the extension of His heart into community form.

In the next chapter, we will turn to Earth—Not-Heaven—and see why a world of danger, loss, and struggle was necessary to form souls fit for the Heaven Jesus established.

Part II Earth and the Vulnerable Soul

Chapter 8 – Why Earth Exists: The Need for a Training Ground

Once Heaven was established – a realm built around shared joy and reverence for the sensibility of others – Jesus faced a profound problem. Heaven was beautiful, but it was unstable. Powerful beings, created in joy, could still fall into indifference. Free will alone was not enough to secure eternal harmony.

Jesus needed a way to form souls who would freely and deeply embrace Heaven's two great commitments:

1. Respect for pain, and
2. Joy of existence shared with others.

This formation required something Heaven could not provide.

Why Heaven Could Not Form Souls

Heaven was too bright, too easy, too immediate. There was little resistance, little limitation, little danger. Without the experience of struggle, humility, and consequence, free beings might celebrate their own joy but fail to honor the inner life of others—just as some angels had done.

In the realm of pure spirit:

❖ no one suffered hunger,

- ❖ no bodies failed,
- ❖ no loss occurred,
- ❖ no vulnerability grounded empathy.

Angels could feel, but they could not be wounded in the ways humans would later be wounded. They lacked the physical and emotional fragility that teaches compassion so deeply. Jesus could see that a deeper morality school was needed, a place where free beings could experience the real cost of indifference and cruelty. But He refused to build that school inside His original world, because there it would have required Him to inflict pain directly on the sensibilities which He had already declared good. To turn Heaven itself into a classroom of deliberate wounding would have corrupted its very nature and His own.

Free will without formative experience proved insufficient. Heaven could not safely absorb another rebellion.

A new realm was needed.

Creating Not-Heaven

Jesus conceived a world utterly unlike Heaven:

- ❖ physical,
- ❖ limited,
- ❖ governed by law and randomness,

❖ indifferent to sensibility,

❖ full of risk, pressure, and uncertainty.

This world would be called Not-Heaven.

It was not a punishment; it was a solution. Jesus designed Earth as a place where souls could grow gradually, responsibly, and safely into beings capable of eternal harmony.

He also knew that creating a world with real danger made Him morally answerable for the suffering that would unfold within it. Even if the blows came from weather, biology, or human choices, they would fall in a system He had chosen to allow. Jesus did not evade that responsibility. From the beginning, He resolved that He would one day enter this world Himself and stand under the same conditions—its injustice, its vulnerability, its pain. The Maker of the curriculum would not remain outside its cost.

In Not-Heaven:

❖ the Urge-to-Create continues its impersonal work,

❖ storms form and dissipate without intention,

❖ bodies suffer and heal,

❖ causes and consequences shape lives,

❖ death sets boundaries on pride,

❖ and pain becomes a teacher.

Not-Heaven is dangerous, but not malicious. It disregards sensibility not out of evil, but because atoms cannot feel.

Why Pain Matters Spiritually

Pain is not the goal of Earth, but it is one of its essential conditions.

Pain gives consciousness:

- depth,
- humility,
- empathy,
- self-knowledge,
- and eventually, respect for the pain of others.

A soul that has been wounded and has learned from that wounding without collapsing into bitterness, becomes capable of genuine compassion. Such a soul becomes safe for Heaven—because it would never again dismiss another being's sensibility.

In this sense, pain is not redemptive on its own, but it prepares the will for redemption.

Why Joy Matters Spiritually

Earth also gives souls fleeting experiences of joy:

- in relationships,

- ❖ in beauty,
- ❖ in meaning,
- ❖ in love,
- ❖ in the simple goodness of existence.

These glimpses are not Heaven, but they are hints of it. They prepare souls for the deeper and more stable joy that defines Jesus' own consciousness.

A soul that knows joy and honors pain is ready for Heaven.

The Curriculum of Earth

Earth is not Heaven, and it was never meant to be. Nor is it Hell, which is a spiritual condition, not a physical place.

Earth is a curriculum, where each soul learns:

- ❖ how to value its own existence,
- ❖ how to value the existence of others,
- ❖ how to care about pain,
- ❖ how to resist indifference,
- ❖ how to choose qualities,
- ❖ how to grow into harmony.

Here, souls make choices with real consequences. They learn by acting, failing, seeking, and persevering. They experience joy and loss, courage and fear, truth and self-deception.

The Purpose of Earth

Earth exists for one reason:

to prepare souls for the Heaven Jesus founded after the rebellion.

Not-Heaven is the forge in which the eternal personality is shaped. No one is forced to become compatible with Heaven, but everyone is invited. Jesus walks within this world, helping each soul interpret its experiences through the lens of qualities.

He does not override the world's natural processes; He accompanies us within them, teaching us how to live spiritually in an arena built from impersonal possibility.

The Decision Ahead

Not-Heaven is temporary. Heaven is permanent.

Earth is the place where souls decide what they want to become. Some choose the path of qualities; others choose indifference. Some awaken to the joy of existence; others remain enclosed in fear or self-focus.

Jesus created Earth not to test us in cruelty, but to prepare us in love.

In the next chapter, we will explore the nature of Not-Heaven itself, and why a world indifferent to sensibility plays such a vital role in forming souls for eternal life.

Chapter 9 – Not-Heaven: Existence Without Regard for Sensibility

When Jesus conceived the need for a place where souls could grow through limitation, vulnerability, and consequence, He did not create a softer version of Heaven. He created something fundamentally different. He created Not-Heaven.

But there was a problem.

A world like this would inevitably contain pain. Bodies would be breakable. Relationships would fracture. Accidents would happen. Storms would not ask permission.

No one born into such a world would have been able to opt out of its conditions. No one would have been asked,

- ❖ "Would you like to exist?" or
- ❖ "Would you like to be formed in a place where you can be hurt?"

They would simply awaken inside the story.

Jesus understood the moral weight of that. If He created a realm where suffering was possible, then every cry of pain would echo inside a system He had chosen to allow. Even if the immediate cause was weather, biology, or human cruelty, the larger frame would still be His. He refused to treat this lightly. He would not become a distant architect of a painful world who remained personally untouched by what it cost its inhabitants to live there.

So He set a boundary for Himself: He would never turn Heaven into a morality school by inflicting pain directly on angels. And if He created Not-Heaven as a training ground for souls, He would one day enter it Himself. The Maker of the curriculum would not stand outside the classroom.

Not-Heaven is not a moral judgment. It is a structural description. It names a kind of world whose processes, conditions, and behaviors do not account for the inner lives of conscious beings. Its winds are blind. Its pressures are indifferent. Its outcomes are not tailored to comfort or avoid suffering. In Not-Heaven, the universe behaves by law, probability, and consequence, not by moral intention.

Jesus knew this indifference would be hard for souls to endure. He also knew it would be the only environment where humility, empathy, courage, and responsibility could become real. So He made Himself a promise: if He allowed a world like this, He would meet every soul inside it. He would not simply watch their Gethsemanes; He would have His own.

Later, in a garden of His own anguish, Jesus would ask His friends, "Stay here and keep watch with Me." He would allow human beings to be with Him in His pain—even when they failed to stay awake. That scene in Gethsemane reveals the shape of His prior commitment: the One who would one day invite us to be with Him in His suffering had already resolved to be with us in ours.

The moral problem of a world with no opt out from vulnerability is not solved by offering an escape from existence. It is answered by the Presence that steps inside existence and refuses its own escape. In creating Not-Heaven, Jesus did not promise to shield us from every wound. He promised something harder and more intimate: to walk within this indifferent creation, alongside each soul, sharing the weight of a world He chose for our formation.

Why Not-Heaven Is Necessary

Not-Heaven trains the soul in ways Heaven cannot:

1. Vulnerability teaches empathy. To suffer is to learn what pain means. To heal is to learn what compassion requires.

2. Consequence teaches responsibility. In a lawful universe, choices have predictable effects. Souls can learn, adjust, and grow.

3. Limitation teaches humility. A being without limits cannot grasp humility. Earth's pressures shape the will.

4. Uncertainty teaches trust. Heaven is clarity. Earth is risk. Trust matures only where outcomes are not guaranteed.

5. Loss teaches value. We learn the worth of joy by its fragility, and the worth of one another by the wound of absence.

In Heaven, these lessons cannot occur. In Not-Heaven, they occur daily.

The Misinterpretation of Suffering

Because Not-Heaven is indifferent, its pains can feel personal. But they are not.

- ❖ Illness is not divine punishment.
- ❖ Accidents are not cosmic messages.
- ❖ Hardship is not designed to "teach a lesson."
- ❖ Disasters are not "God's anger."

This misinterpretation causes needless confusion and spiritual harm.

In SC3, Jesus clarifies:

Creation does not intend your suffering. But I do intend your healing. The UTC does not plan pain. But I use every experience, joyful or painful, as material for spiritual growth—never as a punishment, always as a possibility.

Not-Heaven Is Not Hell

Not-Heaven is often confused with Hell. But they are categorically different:

* Not-Heaven is the physical world's indifference to sensibility.
* Hell is a spiritual condition shaped by a will that disregards the pain of others.

The former is structural. The latter is moral.

* Not-Heaven can wound you accidentally. Hell wounds by chosen coldness.
* Not-Heaven trains you. Hell mirrors you.
* Not-Heaven is temporary. Hell is self-chosen permanence.

Earth: The Soul's Laboratory

Earth sits inside Not-Heaven as a unique environment:

- ❖ dangerous enough to produce vulnerability,
- ❖ lawful enough to produce consequence,
- ❖ uncertain enough to produce trust,
- ❖ relational enough to produce love.

Here, souls discover what they will become:

- ❖ beings capable of Heaven's joy,
- ❖ or beings drifting toward the indifference of Hell.

Jesus walks with us in this world—not to change its indifference, but to change us within it.

Why Jesus Does Not Override Not-Heaven

People often ask why Jesus does not stop storms, diseases, accidents, or tragedies.

In SC3, the answer is simple and dignifying: Because Not-Heaven is the curriculum, not the exam.

If Jesus removed every difficulty,

- ❖ humility could not grow,
- ❖ courage could not rise,
- ❖ mercy could not deepen,
- ❖ empathy would remain shallow,
- ❖ and free will would never mature.

He does not override the curriculum. He walks beside the student. He transforms hearts, not the weather.

But He does more than accompany; He participates. The moral problem of pain in Not-Heaven is not solved by explanation but by participation. Jesus allowed a world where bodies can be wounded and then took one of those bodies for Himself. By accepting crucifixion, He shared the full cost of the system He made, entering suffering not as a supervisor, but as an equal.

Not-Heaven as the Prelude to Heaven

Not-Heaven is not the enemy of Heaven. It is the prelude.

It is the place where souls learn:

- to respect the inner life of others,
- to care about pain,
- to rejoice in being,
- to choose qualities freely,
- to become beings who can share Heaven's eternal joy.

In the next chapter, we will explore the nature of human beings—consciousness embodied in this indifferent creation—and how Jesus uses our experience here to prepare us for the Heaven He founded after the first rebellion.

Chapter 10 – Humans: Embodied Consciousness in a Harsh Arena

When consciousness first appeared in the form of angels, it appeared in a realm of pure spirit. Their existence was luminous, direct, and unburdened by physical limitation. They could perceive one another's presence, respond to the joy of existence, and, in some cases, disregard the pain of others. But they could not yet understand the full weight of vulnerability. They could not feel what it means to be fragile.

To solve the instability revealed by the angelic rebellion, Jesus created a new form of conscious life—one embodied, finite, and bound to the physical conditions of Not-Heaven. Thus emerged the human being: a consciousness in a body, designed not as punishment but as curriculum.

The Human Condition as Curriculum

The human condition is defined by two simultaneous truths:

1. We are conscious "I"s, capable of meaning, choice, reflection, and moral growth.
2. We are embodied, subject to limitation, fatigue, hunger, injury, illness, loss, and death.

This duality is not accidental. It is the very structure that allows human beings to learn what angels could not:

- ❖ humility born of limitation,
- ❖ empathy born of vulnerability,
- ❖ compassion born of personal suffering,
- ❖ gratitude born of impermanence,
- ❖ courage born of facing finitude,
- ❖ and reverence for the inner life of others born from knowing our own.

A disembodied being may ignore pain. An embodied being cannot.

Fragility as Teacher

The body is fragile on purpose.

We scrape, bruise, break, ache, bleed, and eventually return to dust. Our emotions are tender. Our minds are easily wounded. Our hearts can be shattered.

This fragility teaches what raw power cannot teach: the meaning of pain.

A being who has felt pain deeply – and has not collapsed into bitterness – becomes the kind of being who will never again treat another's pain lightly.

In this way, the human condition forms souls who are safe for Heaven.

The Experience of Joy

Human life also brings glimpses of joy:

- ❖ the warmth of relationship,
- ❖ the beauty of nature,
- ❖ the wonder of creativity,
- ❖ the peace of quiet moments,
- ❖ the delight of love freely given.

These joys are not permanent, but they are real. They whisper to us of a deeper joy – the joy Jesus experienced at the first moment of His own consciousness.

In human life, we learn that joy is fragile and therefore precious. We learn that another's joy matters, because we know the sweetness of our own. We learn that shared existence is good and that the world is better when we celebrate one another's being.

This prepares us for a Heaven where joy is stable, not fleeting.

Why Humans Cannot Fully Control Their World

Humans often struggle with the fact that they cannot control Not-Heaven:

- ❖ weather,
- ❖ illness,
- ❖ accidents,
- ❖ natural disasters,
- ❖ aging,
- ❖ and death.

Yet this lack of control is precisely what shapes spiritual maturity. To control everything would be to remain shallow. To live without control teaches humility, trust, and the ability to navigate uncertainty.

In Heaven, all beings are powerful. On Earth, all beings are softened.

Power without humility is dangerous. Humility without power is incomplete. Earth prepares the soul to later hold both without harm.

The Awakening of the Human "I"

Human consciousness matures slowly. Infants do not know they exist as separate beings. Children discover the "I" gradually. Adults refine it over decades.

This slow awakening mirrors Jesus' original awakening, but at a smaller scale. It allows each soul to ask—and eventually answer—the question Jesus answered first:

"What am I?"

In a body, the human soul discovers:

- ❖ "I am not merely my instincts."
- ❖ "I am not merely my emotions."
- ❖ "I am not merely my thoughts."
- ❖ "I am my consciousness."

And when healing deepens:

- ❖ "It is good that I exist."
- ❖ "It is good that others exist."

Learning to Honor the Pain of Others

Human experience is a tapestry of shared vulnerability. We witness one another's suffering:

- ❖ in families,
- ❖ in friendships,
- ❖ in communities,
- ❖ in illness,
- ❖ in heartbreak,
- ❖ in injustice,
- ❖ in loss.

Each moment becomes an invitation:

- ❖ Will I turn away from another's pain?

61

❖ Or will I respond with qualities: love, truth, courage, mercy, humility, harmony?

Each decision forms the soul. Each decision reveals what kind of eternity the soul is becoming fit for.

Humanity as Jesus' Eternal Project

Jesus did not create humans to test them in cruelty. He created humans to form them:

- ❖ to learn empathy through suffering,
- ❖ to learn gratitude through joy,
- ❖ to learn humility through limitation,
- ❖ to learn courage through adversity,
- ❖ to learn love through relationship,
- ❖ to learn harmony through difference.

Earth is not Heaven. Earth is preparation for Heaven.

The Great Dignity of Human Life

To be human is to be a soul in formation – a consciousness learning how to care, how to rejoice, how to become safe for eternity.

Every joy and every sorrow is part of that process. Every success and every failure is material for growth. Every wound and every healing is shaping the inner life for its final home.

In the next chapter, we explore the core polarity of conscious experience – pain and joy – and how this polarity becomes the foundation for spiritual formation on Earth.

Chapter 11 – Pain and Joy: The Two Axes of Conscious Experience

Pain and joy are the first two realities every conscious being must face. Before morality, before religion, before law, before love, before fear – even before choice – there is sensibility: the inner experience of being a conscious "I."

Nothing in the physical universe feels pain or joy. Atoms do not resent collisions. Stars do not appreciate their own beauty. The Urge-to-Create does not tremble at tragedy or rejoice in creation. It is indifferent by nature and must remain so.

Pain and joy arise only when consciousness enters the scene. When beings awaken to themselves, they awaken to meaning.

Jesus' practical method can be stated simply in modern terms: name the weather, name the quality, take the next step. We will return to this method below, and it is summarized in Appendix A (quality equations).

Pain: The Signal of Harm

Pain is the first signal that someone's sensibility has been injured.

It does not matter whether that pain comes from:

❖ physical injury,
❖ emotional disappointment,

- ❖ betrayal,
- ❖ fear,
- ❖ loneliness,
- ❖ or injustice.

Pain always communicates the same fundamental truth:

"Something in me has been hurt."

Pain is not punishment. It is information. Only important things hurt, so pain points to what matters. It reveals vulnerability, limitation, and the delicate structure of the inner life.

Pain is also what gives morality its depth. If a being can feel pain, then its inner life matters. Its well-being has moral weight.

The entire moral universe becomes possible only because pain is real.

Pain also distorts consciousness. Under strong pain the soul can begin to believe that the present wound is the whole truth. The future darkens, effort seems futile, and pain looks permanent. Anxiety can be understood as a variety of pain - pain projected forward, a forecast of hurt, a scanning of the future for danger. Psychology calls part of this effect mood-congruent recall: when the soul hurts, it more easily remembers hurt and expects more hurt.

Trauma often deepens when pain produces objection and retreat. The protest is understandable, but if objection becomes permanent, consciousness remains organized around the wound. Acceptance does not mean calling evil good. It means telling the truth: this hurts, this matters, and pain is not the whole reality. Ending pain is not the same as heavenly joy. Relief matters, but the deeper goal is to cope with pain well enough that the soul can return to purpose, practice love, and rejoin the joy of existence.

Joy: The Signal of Goodness

Joy is the counterpart to pain.

It signals:

* the goodness of being,
* the value of relationship,
* the beauty of existence,
* the rightness of harmony,
* the peace of safety,
* the fulfillment of meaning.

Joy is the spiritual echo of Jesus' first awareness: "It is good that I exist."

Every true joy we taste is a faint reflection of the joy He discovered in His first moment of consciousness.

Joy reveals that the soul is not only capable of suffering. It is capable of perceiving goodness. It is capable of recognizing the value of existence—its own and others'.

Pain and Joy as Moral Compass

Pain and joy are the two axes of conscious existence. Every moral decision touches one or the other:

- Will my choice increase someone's pain?
- Will my choice honor someone's joy?
- Will my action disregard their experience?
- Will my desire contribute to their flourishing or their harm?

Morality in SC3 is built entirely on the recognition of sensibility. The simplest summary is:

Goodness honors the inner life of others; evil disregards it.

Pain is what reveals another's vulnerability. Joy is what reveals another's worth.

Why These Two Axes Matter for Spiritual Growth

Earth is the world where souls learn to navigate pain and joy:

- ❖ to understand their own pain,
- ❖ to see the pain of others,
- ❖ to recognize their own joy,
- ❖ to rejoice in the joy of others,
- ❖ and to become the kind of beings who act from qualities rather than impulses.

Earth is the first school of empathy. It is the first school of gratitude. It is the first school of meaning.

These lessons prepare the soul for Heaven, where:

- ❖ pain is no longer possible,
- ❖ joy is endlessly deepened,
- ❖ and harmony is permanent.

The Purpose of Pain

Pain's purpose is not to punish. Pain teaches:

- ❖ humility,
- ❖ compassion,
- ❖ responsibility,
- ❖ courage,
- ❖ and the sacredness of the inner life.

Souls who have known pain and grown through it are capable of caring for the pain of others. Souls who have never faced pain cannot be trusted with power.

The Purpose of Joy

Joy's purpose is not to distract. Joy teaches:

- gratitude,
- appreciation,
- connection,
- belonging,
- and harmony.

Souls who cherish joy—both their own and others'—are safe for Heaven. Souls who resent others' joy are moving away from Jesus' nature.

The Balance of Heaven

In Heaven, pain is absent, but its lessons remain. Souls who enter Heaven have learned to:

- prevent pain rather than cause it,
- care more than they harm,
- rejoice sincerely in others' existence,
- and contribute to harmony rather than fracture it.

Joy becomes the stable atmosphere of eternity because every soul within it has learned, through Earth's pain and Earth's brief joys, what joy truly means.

The Balance of Hell

Hell is the realm shaped by disregard:

- ❖ disregard for pain,
- ❖ disregard for joy,
- ❖ disregard for the inner life of oneself or others.

Hell is what happens when consciousness chooses indifference. Not-Heaven is indifferent by structure; Hell is indifference by choice.

The Human Task

The human task is to integrate these two axes:

1. Honor pain—both your own and others'—as morally meaningful.
2. Celebrate joy—both your own and others'—as spiritually meaningful.

Jesus teaches us how.

Because pain can look final, faith is especially needed while pain is present. Faith is not denial of hurt. It is the soul's refusal to let pain become the whole truth. It says: light still exists, joy still exists, Jesus is still near, and my wanting still matters.

This is why Jesus so often says, 'Do not be afraid.' He is not belittling pain; He is calling consciousness back from fear's narrowing into the deeper reality that goodness and guidance remain. A distressed child is not healed by being told that nothing hurts, but by being comforted until safety and play become imaginable again. So too the soul before Jesus.

A Simple Practice: Name the Weather, Name the Quality, Take the Next Step

This is the transformative point. Spiritual life is not pain avoidance, and it is not the pursuit of pain. Seeking pain is not a valid spiritual practice. Pain is a contrast to beauty and joy—an alarm that a quality has been violated or threatened. The practice is to become conscious of pain and translate it into quality.

Jesus offered quality words as a method to transform pain. He repeatedly takes what hurts and gives it a higher-quality direction—truth without cruelty, mercy without denial, courage without pride, love without self-protection. Quality words do not erase pain; they reorganize consciousness so the "I" can choose the next faithful action.

Consider the storm at sea. The disciples' weather is fear. Jesus speaks peace, and the waves yield. The deeper lesson is inner governance: name the fear, choose trust, embody calm until the inside matches Heaven's order. Walking on water repeats the same principle—quality stands over chaos.

1) Name the weather: one sentence, no blame (anger, fear, grief, shame, numbness, confusion).

2) Name the quality: what quality is violated—or what quality is needed now (truth, mercy, courage, humility,

72

trust, love).

3) Take the next step: choose one visible action that expresses the quality (question, boundary, apology, clarification, repair, prayer).

For additional quality equations and examples that apply this method under pressure, see Appendix A – Qualities and quality equations.

He is the one who understands both pain and joy perfectly. He invites us to learn the lessons of Earth so we may one day enter the joy of Heaven, having become souls who will never again disregard the inner life of another.

In the next chapter, we will explore how Jesus enters history as the eternal "I" and how He brings His understanding of pain and joy into the human world.

Chapter 12 – Vulnerability: The Path to Heaven

Vulnerability is not the enemy of the spiritual life. Vulnerability is the path by which the soul becomes a citizen of Heaven.

In every moment of vulnerability, the soul is being shaped into the kind of being Jesus can trust with eternity.

This is why Earth cannot be Heaven. Heaven celebrates vulnerability healed; Earth teaches vulnerability experienced.

Vulnerability prepares the soul for joy. Only a soul that has suffered can truly rejoice in the goodness of existence. Only a soul that has felt fear can truly appreciate safety. Only a soul that has known sorrow can truly celebrate love.

Heaven requires beings who can honor the sensibility of others. Vulnerability is how the soul learns to do so.

A soul that rejects vulnerability becomes rigid, proud, defensive, harsh, and spiritually blind. A soul that accepts vulnerability becomes receptive, gentle, truthful, and capable of deep relationship.

Because of vulnerability, human beings can learn mercy. Because of vulnerability, human beings can learn courage. Because of vulnerability, human beings can learn compassion, forgiveness, patience, and love.

Jesus embraced vulnerability to teach us its dignity. He accepted infancy, hunger, fatigue, grief, misunderstanding, and ultimately death. He did not enter the human condition to observe it but to feel it. Every limitation He accepted was a lesson for humanity: vulnerability is not shameful; it is formative.

Vulnerability is also the curriculum of humility. When the soul confronts its limits—physical, emotional, relational, or moral—it is freed from the illusions of superiority or self-sufficiency. Humility is not self-reduction; it is accurate self-perception.

Vulnerability is the curriculum of empathy. It is how the heart becomes able to care genuinely and deeply.

Vulnerability teaches the soul what Heaven requires. When a person suffers loss, disappointment, fear, loneliness, or heartbreak, they come into direct contact with what sensibility is. This awareness is the moral foundation of the soul. A being who has suffered and learned from suffering becomes incapable of ignoring the pain of others.

Humans rise because they are fragile before they are powerful.

Part III Jesus in History and the Transformation of Religion

Chapter 13 – Incarnation: The Eternal "I" Enters History

For ages, Jesus existed as the first Consciousness, the primal "I" who awakened within the Urge-to-Create. He had created angels, quelled rebellion, established Heaven, and designed Earth as the training ground where souls could learn empathy, humility, courage, and the joy of existence. But for human beings to understand Him, He had to do more than whisper to conscience or appear in visions. He had to enter the human condition Himself.

Incarnation was not an afterthought. It was the next necessary step in His project to populate Heaven with souls capable of love, truth, and the reverence for sensibility that keeps Heaven stable forever.

The Eternal "I" Steps Into Flesh

When Jesus entered history in a human body, He did something astonishing: the first Consciousness became an infant. The eternal "I"—who had once stood alone in limitless awareness—accepted limitation, dependence, hunger, cold, and vulnerability.

This was not a disguise. It was a participation.

To guide human beings into Heaven, He had to experience:

- ❖ physical pain,
- ❖ emotional complexity,
- ❖ social pressures,
- ❖ loneliness,
- ❖ misunderstanding,
- ❖ and mortality.

By entering these conditions, He honored the curriculum of Earth. He did not bypass it. He walked it.

Why Incarnation Was Necessary

Words spoken from Heaven could not have taught humans what they most needed to know. We needed someone who had lived in our world, suffered our pain, and yet remained faithful to the qualities that define Heaven.

We needed someone who could show:

- ❖ what love looks like when life is unfair,
- ❖ what truth looks like when it costs something,
- ❖ what courage looks like when danger is real,
- ❖ what mercy looks like when hearts are wounded,
- ❖ what humility looks like when power is available,
- ❖ what harmony looks like when conflict surrounds us.

Jesus did not come to perform spectacle. He came to demonstrate the Heavenly nature inside human limitations.

Jesus' Human Life as Revelation

Every moment of Jesus' life reveals something essential:

- ❖ His compassion shows His integrity: He cannot ignore pain.
- ❖ His teachings show His clarity: He knows the nature of Heaven.
- ❖ His patience shows His gentleness: He will not overwhelm the will.
- ❖ His courage shows His truthfulness: He will not abandon love under pressure.
- ❖ His suffering shows His solidarity: He takes part in the fragility He created for us.
- ❖ He lived the human experience from the inside so that no soul could say:
- ❖ "You do not understand what it is like to be me."

He understands perfectly.

Jesus as Interpreter of Humanity

When Jesus walked the earth, He served as the interpreter of both God and humanity:

- ❖ He interpreted God for humanity by showing that God's heart cares for our pain and celebrates our joy.
- ❖ He interpreted humanity for God by living the human condition from within – bringing the texture of human sensibility into divine experience.

Jesus became the bridge not by theory, but by incarnation.

He learned what hunger feels like. He learned the weight of grief. He learned what it means to be misunderstood. He learned the cost of fidelity in a world that does not understand fidelity.

In doing so, He revealed the true nature of humanity: beings capable of Heaven, if healed.

Incarnation as Alignment, Not Intervention

Jesus did not come to override Earth's processes or abolish Not-Heaven's structure. He came to live within it as we do.

He did not stop storms. He slept in them. He did not prevent sorrow. He wept with those who suffered. He did not escape death. He passed through it.

He did not come to rearrange Earth. He came to rearrange the soul.

The Meaning of "God With Us"

The ancient title "Emmanuel" means "God with us." In SC3 this means:

- ❖ God-as-possibility (UTC) is not personal—but
- ❖ God-as-person (Jesus) is fully with us in every dimension of human experience.

When human beings speak of "God caring," they are speaking—whether they know it or not—of Jesus.

He is God in a form that:

- ❖ sees,
- ❖ feels,
- ❖ chooses,
- ❖ suffers,
- ❖ rejoices,
- ❖ teaches,
- ❖ and loves.

He is the one who understands both Heaven and Earth, both angels and humans, both joy and pain.

The Human Life as Invitation

Jesus' life – His actions, His teachings, His friendships, His griefs, His death, His resurrection – was not meant to be observed from a distance. It was meant to be imitated.

He came into history so that humanity could see Heaven lived out in human form and recognize:

"This is who we are meant to become."

Jesus is not merely the founder of a religion. He is the first fully formed soul, the template for the eternal community, the model of what a human being looks like when fully compatible with Heaven.

The Meaning of the Incarnation for SC3

Incarnation is the hinge of the whole spiritual project:

- Heaven needed stable souls.
- Earth needed a teacher who understood Heaven.
- Humanity needed a guide who understood Earth.
- God needed to be known in a form that respects human consciousness.

Jesus fulfilled all of this by entering history.

He came not only to reveal God, but to reveal humanity to itself— to show us what we are meant to become:

❖ beings who honor pain,

❖ share joy,

❖ live qualities,

❖ and join Him in Heaven as eternal companions.

In the next chapter, we will explore how Jesus' mission unfolded – how He sought to populate Heaven with souls formed through the challenges and opportunities of Earth.

Chapter 14 – The Mission: Populate Heaven With Souls of Qualities

When Jesus entered history, He came with a purpose older than the universe. His earthly ministry was not an improvisation and not merely a response to human failure. It was the continuation of the same mission He began when He first awakened as Consciousness within the Urge-to-Create.

The Heavenly Problem

After the angelic rebellion, Jesus faced a profound truth: Heaven could not be eternally stable unless its inhabitants were beings who:

- understood both joy and pain,
- freely embraced qualities,
- would never again disregard the inner life of another,
- and were capable of rejoicing in one another's existence forever.

Angels were powerful, but power without formation is dangerous. Heaven required beings shaped by experience, humility, empathy, and love.

Jesus needed a way to form souls – gently, slowly, freely.

Why Humanity Became the Solution

To solve this, He created humanity: conscious beings embodied in Not-Heaven, where suffering, joy, limitation, relationship, freedom, and consequence could work together to form a stable, eternal "I."

Human beings become the bridge between Heaven and Earth, the beings who can learn:

- ❖ what pain means,
- ❖ what joy means,
- ❖ what love costs,
- ❖ what truth demands,
- ❖ what courage requires,
- ❖ what mercy heals,
- ❖ what humility protects,
- ❖ how harmony is built.

We are not accidents. We are Jesus' long-term project.

Jesus' Mission on Earth

When Jesus appeared in human form, He came to complete what He began before time:

To populate Heaven with souls who are compatible with Heaven.

He came to:

- ❖ teach qualities,
- ❖ clarify desire,
- ❖ reshape motives,
- ❖ heal pain,
- ❖ correct indifference,
- ❖ and awaken the human "I" to its eternal destiny.

Jesus did not come to found a religion; He came to form a people fit for eternity.

Two Tasks of His Mission

Jesus had two major tasks during His earthly ministry:

1. To teach qualities—Heaven's nature.

These include:

- ❖ Love
- ❖ Truth
- ❖ Courage
- ❖ Mercy
- ❖ Humility
- ❖ Harmony

He taught them not only in words but with His actions, His friendships, His suffering, and His death.

Qualities are not virtues to admire; they are capacities needed to thrive in Heaven.

89

2. To teach how to relate to Himself and the UTC.

Jesus taught us:

* ❖ how to form desire,
* ❖ how to pray without superstition,
* ❖ how to clarify our goals,
* ❖ how to surrender fear,
* ❖ how to live spiritually in an indifferent world,
* ❖ how to trust a God who shapes possibility but does not micromanage events.

He taught: "Ask, and it will be given," meaning: "Shape your intention clearly, morally, and with Me."

He taught: "Your Father knows what you need," meaning: "The Source responds to desire, not anxiety."

He taught: "The Kingdom is within you," meaning: "Heaven begins in consciousness, not geography."

The Type of Beings Heaven Requires

Heaven needs beings who:

* ❖ love without domination,
* ❖ speak truth without cruelty,
* ❖ act with courage without aggression,
* ❖ show mercy without naiveté,
* ❖ walk in humility without self-erasure,

❖ sustain harmony without enforcing uniformity.

These qualities form the soul's eternal identity.

In Jesus, these qualities are perfect. In humanity, they must be learned.

Earth as Soul-Formation

Jesus' mission requires Earth's conditions:

❖ vulnerability teaches compassion,
❖ limitation teaches humility,
❖ uncertainty teaches trust,
❖ suffering teaches empathy,
❖ failure teaches honesty,
❖ joy teaches gratitude,
❖ relationships teach love.

Earth hurts, but it trains. Earth disappoints, but it clarifies. Earth breaks, but it remakes.

Under Jesus' guidance, Earth becomes the furnace of soul-formation.

The Invitation of His Life

Jesus does not demand that we become replicas of Him. He invites us to let Him shape us:

❖ through our desires,

- ❖ our pains,
- ❖ our joys,
- ❖ our relationships,
- ❖ our failures,
- ❖ our hopes,
- ❖ and our prayers.

The invitation is personal: "Follow Me, and I will shape you for Heaven."

The Fulfillment of the Mission

Jesus' mission will be fulfilled when:

- ❖ Heaven is filled with beings who share the joy of existence,
- ❖ beings who honor the sensibility of others,
- ❖ beings who embody the qualities that make eternal community possible,
- ❖ and beings who can live forever in a realm beyond pain because they have learned to respect it deeply.

This is why Jesus came. This is why we are here.

In the next chapter, we will see how Jesus' teachings reveal His heart for human pain and the moral urgency that flows from His own eternal experience of joy.

Chapter 15 – Jesus and the Respect for Pain

When Jesus entered the human world, He did so carrying the deepest insight any conscious being has ever held: that pain is morally significant. This insight did not begin in Bethlehem. It began in the earliest moments of His existence as the first Consciousness, long before Earth, long before angels, long before the rebellion.

To understand Jesus' teaching, we must understand this: Jesus cannot ignore pain. His very nature makes that impossible.

Where Jesus Learned the Weight of Pain

As the first "I," Jesus experienced the joy of existence—pure being, unclouded and good. But once He created angels—other conscious beings capable of joy—He encountered something new: their vulnerability.

Where there is consciousness, there can be hurt. Where there is hurt, there is moral weight.

This realization shaped Jesus' entire understanding of good and evil.

When some angels began to disregard the pain of others—treating others inner lives as negligible—Jesus saw the birth of evil. Not in violence, not in open malice, but in indifference.

Evil begins with: "Your pain does not matter to me."

Goodness begins with: "Your inner life matters."

Jesus' Moral Instinct

Jesus' instinct is always the same:

- ❖ If someone suffers, He notices.
- ❖ If someone is frightened, He cares.
- ❖ If someone is wounded, He responds.
- ❖ If someone is ignored, He moves toward them.
- ❖ If someone is mistreated, He is troubled.

This is not a role He performs; it is who He is.

His respect for sensibility is the foundation of all His teachings.

Jesus in Human Form: Pain Up Close

When Jesus entered human life, He submitted Himself to:

- ❖ hunger,
- ❖ fear,
- ❖ misunderstanding,
- ❖ exhaustion,
- ❖ betrayal,
- ❖ grief,
- ❖ and physical agony.

He did not do this to prove something; He did it to participate in the reality He asks us to live in.

By feeling human pain, He demonstrated that:

- ❖ our suffering is real,
- ❖ our tears are meaningful,
- ❖ our wounds matter,
- ❖ our vulnerability is sacred.

He lived what He teaches: that pain is morally important and cannot be dismissed.

Jesus' Response to Human Pain

Throughout His ministry, Jesus consistently acted from respect for sensibility:

- ❖ He touched the sick rather than avoiding them.
- ❖ He fed the hungry rather than preaching at them.
- ❖ He defended the outcast rather than condemning them.
- ❖ He dignified sinners rather than humiliating them.
- ❖ He wept with the grieving rather than offering platitudes.
- ❖ He comforted children rather than ignoring their fear.

Every gesture said the same thing: "Your pain matters to Me."

This was not sentimentality. It was theology lived out in flesh.

Why Jesus' Teaching Harshly Condemns Indifference

Because Jesus' moral universe is built around sensibility, He is hardest on those who show indifference:

- ❖ "Woe to you, scribes and Pharisees..."
- ❖ "You shut the door of Heaven in people's faces..."
- ❖ "You neglect the weightier matters of the law: justice, mercy, and faithfulness."
- ❖ "Whatever you did not do for the least of these, you did not do for Me."

His criticism is reserved for those who refuse to see another's inner life.

For Jesus:

- ❖ cruelty is evil,
- ❖ but indifference is its root.

The failure to notice pain is the soil in which all spiritual corruption grows.

The Cross as the Ultimate Revelation of His Respect

The cross is not Jesus glorifying pain. The cross is Jesus entering the deepest human agony to prove, once for all:

- ❖ that no human suffering is beneath Him,
- ❖ that He will descend to any depth to accompany a soul,
- ❖ and that love is defined by willingness to bear the weight of another's pain.

What Jesus could not tolerate in the angels' rebellion—disregard for pain—He heals in humanity through His own suffering.

Human Pain as Jesus' Concern

In SC3, every experience of pain has moral and spiritual significance because:

- ❖ it reveals vulnerability,
- ❖ it awakens empathy,
- ❖ it teaches humility,
- ❖ it forms character,
- ❖ and it draws Jesus close.

No pain is meaningless. No pain is unnoticed. No pain is wasted.

Pain teaches the soul to care. And a soul that cares is safe for Heaven.

The Two Moral Questions Jesus Asks

Every moral choice centers on two questions:

97

1. Do you honor the pain of another?
2. Do you rejoice in their existence?

A soul that answers "yes" becomes compatible with Heaven. A soul that repeatedly answers "no" moves toward the indifference that forms Hell.

Why Jesus Respects Our Pain More Than We Respect Our Own

We often:

❖ minimize,

❖ repress,

❖ deny,

❖ or shame ourselves for hurting.

Jesus never does.

He sees pain clearly—ours and others'. He sees how deeply it shapes the inner life. He knows that a soul that has not understood its own pain will struggle to understand anyone else's.

So Jesus brings healing not by erasing pain but by illuminating it, honoring it, and transforming it.

Pain as the Teacher of Heaven

Pain is not the foundation of Heaven; joy is. But pain is the teacher that prepares the soul for joy.

A being who has learned:

- ❖ to respect pain,
- ❖ to respond with qualities,
- ❖ to protect the inner life of others,

cannot destabilize Heaven.

This is why Jesus came. This is why He heals. This is why His teachings are so severe against indifference.

Heaven is a home for beings who have learned two deep truths:

Pain must be honored. Joy must be shared.

In the next chapter, we will see how Jesus extends not only respect for pain, but the joy of existence itself— inviting souls to share the gladness that first filled His own consciousness

Chapter 16 – Jesus and the Joy of Existence

If Jesus' relationship to pain reveals His moral center, His relationship to joy reveals His origin. Before angels, before Heaven, before the rebellion, before Earth, Jesus— awakening as the first Consciousness— experienced something profound and peaceful:

The joy of existence.

This joy was not pleasure, not triumph, not excitement. It was the quiet, unshakeable affirmation: "It is good that I exist."

Everything in His nature flows from this joy. It is the beginning of Heaven. It is the heart of His teachings. It is the destiny He intends for every soul.

Jesus' First Joy

When Jesus emerged as the first "I" in the midst of the Urge-to-Create, His awareness opened without fear, without shame, without competition, without comparison.

There was simply:

❖ consciousness,
❖ identity,
❖ being,
❖ and the goodness of being.

101

This inner clarity—joy without ego—became the core of His nature. It shaped every future act of creation: angels, Heaven, Earth, and humanity.

Joy as the Foundation of Heaven

Heaven is not a reward for good behavior. It is the extension of Jesus' first joy into community form.

Heaven's atmosphere is:

* shared delight,
* mutual appreciation,
* the gladness of existence itself.

Every soul in Heaven can say without hesitation:

"It is good that I exist." "It is good that you exist." "And it is good that we exist together."

This is the joy that keeps Heaven stable. This is the joy Jesus wants every soul to know.

Why Joy Must Be Shared

The joy of existence is not solitary. Joy that is hoarded becomes pride. Joy that excludes becomes envy. Joy that turns inward becomes distortion.

Jesus' joy is relational. By its very nature, it seeks reflection.

This is why He created angels—beings capable of reflecting and sharing this joy. It is why He created humans—beings capable of learning this joy through vulnerability, courage, and love.

Heaven grows from shared joy; Hell grows from isolated self-absorption.

Joy and Moral Clarity

Joy and morality are not separate for Jesus.

Because He knows the goodness of existence so deeply, He cannot tolerate anything that injures another's capacity for that joy.

His teaching is not abstract morality; it is practical joy-protection:

- Love protects joy.
- Truth protects joy.
- Courage protects joy.
- Mercy protects joy.
- Humility protects joy.
- Harmony protects joy.

Qualities are not virtues to admire; they are the building blocks of eternal joy. They are how conscious beings sustain the joy of existence together.

Joy and the Ministry of Jesus

Throughout His human life, Jesus' actions reveal His commitment to restoring joy:

- ❖ He heals bodies so joy can return.
- ❖ He forgives sins so shame will not crush joy.
- ❖ He blesses children because their joy is pure.
- ❖ He invites the weary to rest so joy has space to grow.
- ❖ He celebrates meals with friends, revealing that joy is sacred, not trivial.

Even His sorrow – His tears at Lazarus' tomb, His grief over Jerusalem – shows His sensitivity to anything that destroys joy.

Where joy is wounded, He is moved. Where joy is restored, He rejoices.

Joy and the Cross

The cross was agony, but beneath it ran the same eternal truth:

Jesus never lost sight of the goodness of existence, even as He endured the worst of Not-Heaven.

His love for humanity drew Him into suffering. His joy of existence carried Him through it.

The resurrection is not only triumph over death; it is the vindication of joy.

It declares:

"Existence is good, even when death tries to deny it."

Joy in Us

Every glimpse of joy we taste on Earth— beauty, love, peace, connection, wonder— is a faint echo of Jesus' first joy.

We sense it when:

❖ we feel deeply known,
❖ we experience forgiveness,
❖ we laugh without fear,
❖ we love without caution,
❖ we see beauty without possessiveness.

These moments remind us of our origin and our destiny.

The Human Calling to Joy

Our calling is not only to avoid causing pain. Our calling is to grow capable of joy—the kind of joy that can be shared forever.

This means:

* healing our wounds,
* shedding shame,
* choosing qualities,
* caring about others' inner lives,
* and letting Jesus reshape our desires.

He wants us to become beings who can say:

"It is good that I exist." "It is good that you exist."

And mean it in the depth of our being.

The Divine Invitation

Jesus invites every soul into the joy that filled Him before time began.

Heaven is not built from rule-keeping. Heaven is built from joy—joy that respects pain, joy that honors life, joy that delights in others.

This is the joy Jesus lived, the joy He taught, the joy He died to preserve, and the joy He now extends to every soul who follows Him.

In the next chapter, we will explore the four stages of religion and how Jesus leads humanity from rule-based morality to a life grounded in qualities and the Source of joy itself.

Chapter 17 – Stage One: Rules as Protectors of Pain

We now turn from Jesus Himself to how humans respond to Him in stages of religion.

Religion begins with rules because rules are the first and simplest way to protect conscious beings from harm. Before philosophy, before theology, before qualities, before spiritual maturity, humanity's earliest moral insights took the form of direct boundaries:

"Do not do this, because it causes pain."

These early rules are not primitive—they are foundational. They mark the moment when a community recognizes the moral significance of sensibility: that conscious beings can be hurt, and that harm must be restrained.

The First Purpose of Rules: To Prevent Pain

Every moral code begins by identifying actions that reliably injure sensibility:

- killing,
- stealing,
- lying,
- betrayal,
- exploitation,
- violence,

❖ cruelty,

❖ indifference to need.

Rules draw a bright line around these harms and say: "Do not cross this line."

This is the function of the Ten Commandments, the 613 mitzvot, and the earliest moral traditions of every nation.

Rules arise whenever a community experiences the pain that evil causes.

Rules Are Earth's First Form of Mercy

Rules are not about control. They are about protection.

Before there was empathy, before there was compassion, before there was moral reasoning, there was pain.

Rules are the human response to that pain.

They say:

❖ We have suffered from these behaviors."
❖ "We will not allow them to continue."
❖ "We will protect one another."

Even harsh early laws were attempts—imperfect attempts—to restrain cruelty and chaos.

Rules Are Blunt Tools, Not Final Wisdom

Rules operate at the behavioral level:

- ❖ Do not murder.
- ❖ Do not steal.
- ❖ Do not bear false witness.
- ❖ Do not commit adultery.

But rules cannot see motives or desires. They cannot evaluate intention. They cannot discern the heart.

Rules prevent the worst harm, but they cannot produce the best good.

They stop evil; they do not generate love.

Rules are like scaffolding: necessary, but not the building itself.

Rules Are Universally Recognizable

Every civilization, no matter how ancient, has discovered:

- ❖ that killing destabilizes community,
- ❖ that theft destroys trust,
- ❖ that dishonesty fractures relationship,
- ❖ that betrayal wounds the soul,
- ❖ that violence begets violence.

This universality comes from a shared recognition:

Pain is real, and harm spreads.

Religion, at its first stage, responds by naming harmful actions and prohibiting them.

The Ten Commandments as a Map of Pain

The Ten Commandments can be read as a map of how human beings injure each other:

- Murder destroys a life.
- Adultery destroys a covenant.
- Theft destroys security.
- False witness destroys justice.
- Coveting destroys inner peace and fuels resentment.

Each commandment answers a real historical injury.

They reflect the earliest spiritual insight:

"We must not treat others' pain lightly."

Why Jesus Began With Rules

When Jesus taught, He did not discard rules. He blessed them by clarifying their purpose.

He said:

- ❖ "I did not come to abolish the law but to fulfill it."
- ❖ "The Sabbath was made for humanity, not humanity for the Sabbath."
- ❖ "These are the weightier matters: justice, mercy, and faithfulness."

Jesus knew that rules are necessary—but incomplete.

Rules restrain evil, but they cannot transform hearts.

They cannot produce joy of existence. They cannot create Heaven's nature within a soul.

Stage One Is Meant to Be Outgrown

Rules are the beginning of religion, not the end.

They prepare the ground. They create space for conscience. They give early structure to human moral intuition. They prevent the worst forms of harm.

But eventually, the soul must grow beyond rule-keeping into wisdom, into qualities, into love.

Just as a child must learn rules before understanding reasons, humanity had to learn rules before understanding the deeper moral logic.

Stage One teaches: Pain matters. Therefore rules matter.

Stage Two will ask: Why does pain matter? What does suffering reveal about the inner life of conscious beings?

In the next chapter, we explore the second stage of religion: the discovery of the deeper reasons behind the rules.

Chapter 18 – Stage Two: Reasons for the Rules

Rules are the first step in moral and spiritual development, but they are not the last. A rule tells you what not to do. Stage Two asks a deeper question:

"Why must I not do this?"

This is the beginning of moral reasoning, of spiritual reflection, of understanding the inner life of others. It is the moment when religion matures beyond command into meaning.

From Prohibition to Understanding

A child obeys because a parent says, "Don't touch the fire." An adult understands why fire burns.

Likewise, early religion says, "Do not harm." Stage Two asks, "What does harm mean? What does it do to a soul?"

This movement from obedience to insight forms the second stage of religion.

The Pain Beneath Every Rule

Behind every early rule lies a story of suffering:

* Murder destroys a family and fractures a community.
* Theft destroys security and breeds fear.

113

- ❖ Adultery destroys trust and breaks hearts.
- ❖ False witness destroys justice and fuels injustice.
- ❖ Envy destroys inner peace and seeds conflict.

Stage Two begins when we see:

"This rule exists because someone was hurt."

The law becomes a window into human vulnerability.

Compassion Begins With Understanding

When we begin to grasp the reason for the rule, a new kind of morality emerges.

We begin to understand:

- ❖ why betrayal wounds,
- ❖ why cruelty scars,
- ❖ why dishonesty poisons,
- ❖ why neglect crushes,
- ❖ why indifference isolates.

The soul begins to care not only about obedience, but about impact.

Rules prevent harm. Understanding reveals why harm matters.

The Prophets and Stage Two

This is the stage of the prophets, who ask:

- ❖ What does the Lord require of you but to do justice, love mercy, and walk humbly?"
- ❖ "I desire mercy, not sacrifice."
- ❖ "Is this not the fast I choose: to break the chains of injustice?"

The prophets insist:

The reason for the rules is human well-being. The reason for the rules is the inner life.

They oppose empty obedience without compassion.

Jesus and the Advancement Beyond Rules

Jesus stands firmly in Stage Two as He prepares humanity for something higher.

He teaches:

- ❖ "The Sabbath was made for man."
- ❖ "Do not burden people with heavy loads."
- ❖ "Woe to you... you neglect the weightier matters of the law."
- ❖ "Whatever you do to the least of these, you do to Me."

Every one of these teachings points to the same truth:

Rules exist to protect sensibility. They exist to honor the pain and the joy of conscious beings.

The Question Stage Two Asks

At this level, religion asks: "How does my action affect the inner life of another?"

This is where empathy begins. This is where moral imagination awakens. This is where the soul learns to see beyond behavior into consequence.

The Limits of Stage Two

Stage Two reveals moral logic, but still has limits:

- ❖ It can explain why lying is harmful, but it cannot yet teach how to live in truth.
- ❖ It can explain why cruelty is wrong, but not yet how to become merciful.
- ❖ It can explain why violence destabilizes community, but not yet how to build harmony.

Stage Two is moral understanding, not moral transformation.

It prepares the soil of the heart for Stage Three: qualities.

A soul may understand why harm is wrong, yet still cause it. Knowledge alone does not create goodness.

Stage Two generates insight but not transformation. It teaches why the law matters, but not how to embody the heart behind it.

To become a being compatible with Heaven, the soul must move beyond:

- ❖ rule-keeping, and
- ❖ understanding,
- ❖ into something far deeper:

Living from qualities.

This is Stage Three.

In the next chapter, we explore how qualities reveal the spiritual essence behind every rule and every moral insight.

Chapter 19 – Stage Three: The Quality of Rules

Rules restrain harm. Understanding explains why harm is wrong. But qualities reveal what a soul must become in order to live in Heaven.

Stage Three is the shift from external guidance to internal formation. It is the stage where the soul stops asking:

"What does the rule say?" and begins asking:

"What kind of person must I be?"

The Emergence of Qualities

Qualities are not rules. They are not behaviors. They are not virtues in the traditional sense.

They are modes of being:

- ❖ Love
- ❖ Truth
- ❖ Courage
- ❖ Mercy
- ❖ Humility
- ❖ Harmony

These are the qualities that define Jesus' own consciousness. They are the structure of Heaven. They are the moral and spiritual DNA of eternity.

119

- ❖ A rule prevents harm. A quality produces goodness.
- ❖ A rule says, "Do not wound." A quality says, "Heal."
- ❖ A rule says, "Do not lie." A quality says, "Live in truth."
- ❖ A rule says, "Do not hate." A quality says, "Love."

Jesus and the Rise of Qualities

When Jesus taught, He moved humanity decisively into Stage Three.

He said: "You have heard it said... but I say to you..."

- ❖ "Blessed are the merciful..."
- ❖ "Love your enemies..."
- ❖ "Forgive seventy times seven..."
- ❖ "The pure in heart shall see God."
- ❖ "Be peacemakers."

He revealed that morality cannot rely on rules alone. It must arise from the inner disposition of the soul.

Rules regulate behavior. Qualities regulate will.

The Weightier Matters

In His harshest critique of religious leadership, Jesus said:

"You neglect the weightier matters of the law: justice, mercy, and faithfulness."

He did not say the rules were unimportant. He said the qualities behind them were what truly mattered.

For Jesus, a soul that keeps the rules but lacks qualities is not safe for Heaven.

The Structure of Spiritual Maturity

Spiritual maturity is not measured by how strictly one observes rules, nor by how well one understands moral logic, but by how deeply one embodies qualities.

A soul formed in qualities:

- loves without controlling,
- tells the truth without cruelty,
- acts with courage without domination,
- shows mercy without naiveté,
- lives humility without self-erasure,
- builds harmony without suppressing difference.

Such a soul is compatible with Heaven because it mirrors the consciousness of Jesus.

The Failure of Pure Rule-Keeping

Rule-keeping alone can produce:

- ❖ pride ("I obey more than others"),
- ❖ hypocrisy ("I appear righteous but hide darkness"),
- ❖ harshness ("I enforce rules without compassion"),
- ❖ legalism ("I protect the rule rather than the person"),
- ❖ blindness ("I do not see the suffering rules create").

This is why Jesus confronted religious leaders who had elevated rules above qualities.

They had lost sight of the rules' original purpose: to protect sensibility, not to burden it.

The Shift Toward the Heart

Stage Three centers on the heart:

- ❖ not the physical heart,
- ❖ not the emotional heart,
- ❖ but the quality-bearing center of the soul.

In this inner center, the soul decides how to treat others. It is here that Jesus focuses His teaching.

He does not merely want obedient people. He wants transformed people—souls who carry His nature.

Qualities as Heaven's Prerequisite

A soul without qualities cannot remain in Heaven:

❖ Love protects joy.
❖ Truth protects trust.
❖ Courage protects justice.
❖ Mercy protects dignity.
❖ Humility protects community.
❖ Harmony protects peace.

Qualities make Heaven possible. Without them, eternity collapses into pride, rivalry, and conflict.

Jesus teaches qualities not as moral ideals, but as the conditions of eternal life.

The Soul's Movement Toward Qualities

This is the key insight of Stage Three:

Rules restrain outward harm, understanding restrains inner ignorance, but qualities transform the will.

They turn the soul toward Heaven.

A soul that grows in qualities begins to say:

"I want to become someone who... ...loves, ...tells the truth, ...forgives, ...shows mercy, ...brings harmony, ... protects the vulnerable, ...and rejoices sincerely in the existence of others."

This is the soul Jesus seeks to form.

Stage Three prepares the soul for Stage Four: the discovery of the source of qualities, and the recognition that all goodness flows from Jesus' own eternal consciousness.

In the next chapter, we turn to this deepest level of religion.

Chapter 20 – Stage Four: The Source of Qualities

Rules restrain harm. Understanding reveals why harm matters. Qualities transform the soul into a being who freely acts from love, truth, courage, mercy, humility, and harmony.

But none of this becomes complete until the soul discovers the Source of qualities.

Stage Four of religion is the moment when morality becomes spirituality—when the soul realizes that qualities are not just good ideas, not just virtues, not just admirable traits, but expressions of a Person whose consciousness is the fountain of all goodness.

That Person is Jesus.

The Source of Love

Love is not merely an emotion or an ideal. It is the way Jesus experiences the existence of others.

In His first moment of self-awareness, Jesus tasted the joy of existence. That joy naturally extended outward into love—the desire for others to share that joy.

Love originates in Him.

All real love mirrors His first joy: "It is good that you exist."

The Source of Truth

Truth is not merely accuracy or correctness. Truth is clarity, the alignment of consciousness with what is real.

Jesus is the first being who ever knew Himself without distortion. He is the first Consciousness who never lied to Himself.

Truth flows from His nature as the One who sees reality as it is.

When we live in truth, we are living in Him.

The Source of Courage

Courage is not fearlessness. Courage is the willingness to act in harmony with love and truth despite fear.

Jesus is the source of courage because He entered Not-Heaven and endured what we fear: misunderstanding, rejection, suffering, death.

He showed that courage is not a performance but a commitment to the qualities He embodies.

The Source of Mercy

Mercy is not leniency. Mercy is the refusal to let another's pain isolate them.

Jesus embodies mercy because He cannot ignore suffering. He entered human fragility not to punish but to heal.

Mercy flows from His heart because He sees each inner life as precious.

The Source of Humility

Humility is not self-erasure. Humility is the joy of being oneself without comparison.

Jesus is humility because He does not need to dominate to be Himself. He does not need to be worshipped to be whole.

His identity rests securely in the joy of existence He discovered at the beginning.

Humility flows from self-understanding.

The Source of Harmony

Harmony is not the absence of conflict. It is the creation of unity through qualities.

Jesus establishes harmony because He aligns all things with the joy and care that define Heaven.

Harmony is the natural expression of His consciousness in community form.

Why Qualities Require a Person

Qualities are not abstract. They are relational. They require a being who lives them.

A world of rules can function without a personal God. But a world of qualities cannot.

The soul cannot learn:

* ❖ to love without seeing love lived,
* ❖ to forgive without seeing forgiveness lived,
* ❖ to speak truth without seeing truth lived,
* ❖ to act with courage without seeing courage lived.

Jesus is the living embodiment of qualities because He is their Source. They flow from His first joy and His eternal compassion.

Why Stage Four Is the Fulfillment of Religion

* ❖ Stage One says: "Do not harm."
* ❖ Stage Two says: "Understand why harm is wrong."
* ❖ Stage Three says: "Become a person who acts from qualities."
* ❖ Stage Four says: "These qualities come from Jesus, and they lead back to Him."

Religion reaches its fulfillment when the soul recognizes:

128

Goodness is personal. Goodness has a face. Goodness has a voice. Goodness has a will. Goodness is Jesus.

This is why Jesus says:

- ❖ "I am the way, the truth, and the life."
- ❖ "I am the light of the world."
- ❖ "He who has seen Me has seen the Father."

He is not claiming monopoly. He is revealing identity.

He is the first Consciousness in whom goodness became a Self.

A Word About "the Father"

When Jesus called God "Father," His listeners did not imagine a male deity reproducing or a divine family in the human sense. In the Judaism of His time, "Father in heaven" was already a known metaphor: God as the One who formed Israel, sustained them, and exercised gentle authority over them. Jesus did not invent this language; He intensified it. He spoke of "Abba, Father" out of personal intimacy, not biology. In SC3 terms, He was not describing a cosmic male parent standing beside the UTC. He was giving relational language to what the UTC feels like from the inside of His own consciousness—source, security, and shared joy. His audience would have understood "Father" as a warm, covenantal image, not a literal description of how God "produces" children.

The Gospels make a point of saying that Joseph was not the source of Jesus' being. But when Jesus speaks of "my Father," He is not inviting His hearers into a biological puzzle; He is inviting them into His way of relating to the Source. "Father" is not a metaphysical map; it is a relational doorway.

Jesus' mission—to form souls of qualities for Heaven—does not depend on us sorting out metaphysical family trees. His work is to show us what the Father is like in a way we can see, hear, and imitate. That is why He can say, "Whoever has seen Me has seen the Father." The Father does not step onto the stage with independent speeches and actions; the Father's heart is revealed in Jesus' own life.

What This Means for Spirituality

Spirituality becomes coherent only when qualities lead the soul back to their Source.

- ❖ Love without Jesus becomes sentiment.
- ❖ Truth without Jesus becomes cruelty.
- ❖ Courage without Jesus becomes domination.
- ❖ Mercy without Jesus becomes enabling.
- ❖ Humility without Jesus becomes self-rejection.
- ❖ Harmony without Jesus becomes suppression.

With Jesus, qualities become balanced and complete. Apart from Him, they fracture.

The Soul's Response to the Source

The soul that reaches Stage Four begins to say:

- ❖ "I want to become like Him."
- ❖ "I want His qualities to shape my qualities."
- ❖ "I want His consciousness to inform my consciousness."
- ❖ "I want His joy to become my joy."
- ❖ "I want to join the Heaven He created."

Stage Four is not worship in the old sense—fearful obedience before a cosmic ruler. Stage Four is recognition:

"He is the Source of what I most deeply desire to become."

The End of Religion and the Beginning of Relationship

When the soul reaches this stage, religion changes:

- ❖ Rules become irrelevant, except as training wheels.
- ❖ Reasons become background.
- ❖ Qualities become natural.
- ❖ Jesus becomes central.

This is the moment when religion ends and relationship begins.

Stage Four is the moment when the soul understands that the goodness it seeks comes from the One whose joy of existence became the foundation of Heaven.

In the next chapter, we will explore how souls at the earlier stages of religion are helped to recognize the beauty of qualities before they can live from them.

Chapter 20A – From Rules to Qualities: Helping Early-Stage Souls Appreciate the Good

Once the four stages of religion are named, a practical question immediately arises. If Stage Three is the emergence of qualities, how does a soul living at Stage One or Stage Two actually cross that threshold? It is not enough to tell such a soul, "Choose qualities." Early-stage souls rarely perceive qualities first as spiritual beauty. They perceive commands, consequences, reasons, examples, and visible fruit. If qualities are to become real to them, they must become visible before they become lovable, and lovable before they become stable.

This developmental fact is not a defect in religion. It is part of Jesus' gentleness. He does not ask a soul to admire what it has not yet learned to see. Stage One protects the soul through rules. Stage Two deepens the soul through reasons. But if the movement stops there, the person may remain obedient and even thoughtful while never becoming inwardly attracted to mercy, humility, patience, faith, or truthfulness as beautiful ways of being.

Why Rules and Reasons Are Not Enough

Rules restrain harm. Reasons explain why harm matters. Both are necessary. Neither, by itself, produces love of qualities. A person may keep rules out of fear, habit, or social expectation. A person may understand reasons for the rules and still remain spiritually external, asking only, "What should I do?" or "Why is this wise?" without yet asking, "What quality is shining here?"

Stage Three begins when the soul stops treating goodness merely as demand or explanation and begins to sense its beauty. Humility is no longer only useful. Mercy is no longer only reasonable. Faith is no longer only required. They begin to appear desirable. The soul starts to say, "I want to become that kind of person."

The Hidden Need of Stage One and Stage Two

Souls in the earlier stages often need help appreciating qualities because qualities are more subtle than rules. A rule can be stated plainly. A reason can be explained logically. But a quality must be noticed in lived form. It must be embodied in a person, or seen in the fruit it creates, before the soul can admire it. The guide, teacher, pastor, or parent therefore has a developmental task: not only to command and explain, but to reveal the quality hidden inside the command and the explanation.

The earlier stages therefore need assistance in three directions. They need help noticing the good fruit produced by a rule. They need help naming the quality that made that fruit possible. And they need help connecting that quality to Jesus, so that the quality is not left as a mere abstraction but recognized as a participation in His own life.

How Qualities Become Visible

Qualities become visible when they are embodied, fruitful, and named. A child may not admire patience as an abstraction but can see the peace created when anger does not rule a room. A believer may not yet love humility as a quality but can see the growth that becomes possible when correction is received without self-defense. A wounded person may not yet desire mercy but can see the healing that begins when retaliation stops.

In this sense, Stage Three usually grows out of interpreted experience. The rule is kept. The fruit appears. Someone names the quality that made that fruit possible. The soul begins to recognize that what it first obeyed from necessity now deserves admiration. This is how qualities move from invisibility to appreciation.

The Bridge From Obedience to Admiration

The developmental bridge can be stated in a sequence of simple formulas:

        rule + concrete example = visible quality
        rule + repetition = habit
        habit + noticed fruit = respect for the rule
        reason + reflection on the fruit = recognition of the quality
        recognized quality + admiration = appreciation of the quality
        appreciated quality + practice = beginning virtue
        virtue + awareness of Jesus = communion

The same bridge can be stated even more compactly:

        command + action = obedience
        obedience + good fruit = meaning

meaning + named quality = appreciation

appreciation + Jesus = discipleship

These are not mechanical laws. They are developmental descriptions. They show how a soul often moves from external guidance into inward love of the good.

One Human Struggle, Read Through Four Levels

The same human difficulty can be read through all four levels. Once this is seen, the path of development becomes much clearer.

Faith

Stage One: anxiety + pray before reacting = steadier behavior

Stage Two: steadier behavior + noticing God's care = appreciation of faith

Stage Three: anxiety + faith = stability

Stage Four: anxiety + awareness of Jesus' presence = peace

Mercy

Stage One: offense + no retaliation = restrained harm

Stage Two: restrained harm + preserved relationship = appreciation of mercy

Stage Three: offense + mercy = forgiveness

Stage Four: offense + awareness of Jesus' mercy = reconciliation

Humility

Stage One: correction + no self-defense = teachable response

Stage Two: teachable response + seeing growth = appreciation of humility

Stage Three: weakness + humility = growth

Stage Four: humility + following Jesus = likeness to Christ

Patience

Stage One: delay + no grumbling = restrained response

Stage Two: restrained response + seeing good timing = appreciation of patience

Stage Three: waiting + patience = endurance

Stage Four: waiting + trust in Jesus = restful hope

Truthfulness

Stage One: pressure + tell the truth = honest speech
Stage Two: honest speech + growing trust = appreciation of integrity
Stage Three: speech + truthfulness = integrity
Stage Four: speech + abiding in Jesus the Truth = freedom

These examples show that the stages do not contradict one another. They deepen one another. Stage One gives behavioral form. Stage Two gives moral meaning. Stage Three gives beauty and character. Stage Four gives personhood and communion.

Teaching Early-Stage Souls Without Contempt

The guide must never despise Stage One or Stage Two. Rules are merciful. Reasons are illuminating. They are not enemies of maturity; they are its early guardians. The error is not in having rules or reasons, but in mistaking them for the whole of spiritual life.

What helps an earlier-stage soul most is not mockery, but interpretation. Do not only say, "Do not lie." Also say, "Truthfulness makes a soul safe." Do not only say, "Forgive." Also say, "Mercy prevents pain from becoming isolation." Do not only say, "Be patient." Also say, "Patience protects love from the violence of haste." In this way the soul begins to see the quality protected by the rule and the beauty released by the quality.

A teacher who wants Stage One and Stage Two souls to grow should therefore do four things repeatedly: name the rule, explain the reason, point out the fruit, and identify the quality shining through the fruit. The soul then begins to admire what it once merely obeyed.

Why Jesus Remains the Fulfillment

Even when qualities become visible and beloved, the journey is not complete. Qualities are not final abstractions. They are living expressions of Jesus' own consciousness. Stage Four therefore does not abolish the earlier stages; it gathers them into relationship. Rules become intelligible because they protect what Jesus loves. Reasons become luminous because they reveal what His heart sees. Qualities become magnetic because they are recognized as His nature.

The mature soul therefore reads the whole progression in one movement: rules protect pain, reasons reveal meaning, qualities show beauty, and Jesus makes beauty personal. This is why the spiritual guide must never stop at moral explanation. The aim is not only informed behavior, but personal likeness to Christ.

The Master Pattern

The whole developmental movement can be summarized in four lines:

> Stage One: struggle + commanded practice = guarded life
> Stage Two: struggle + understood good = wise life
> Stage Three: struggle + quality = formed character
> Stage Four: struggle + Jesus' presence = communion and fruit

Read horizontally, these formulas show how one difficulty can be interpreted at increasing depth. Read vertically, they show what each stage most needs. For extended formula assemblies organized by quality, see Appendix C.

In the next chapter, we will explore religion as the work of human beings—how humanity's earliest attempts at understanding sensibility, pain, joy, and goodness prepared the way for Jesus' revelation of qualities and their Source.

Chapter 21 – Religion as Human Work

Religion did not begin as a divine decree. It began as the human interpretation of pain, joy, mystery, and the longing for meaning. Long before humanity understood qualities, long before anyone understood the nature of Jesus or the Urge-to-Create, people saw that life hurts, that life delights, and that life demands response.

Religion is humanity's earliest attempt to make sense of consciousness.

Religion Begins With Human Questions

Human beings looked at the world and asked:

- ❖ Why do we suffer?
- ❖ Why do storms come?
- ❖ Why do people die?
- ❖ What causes joy?
- ❖ What protects us?
- ❖ What holds the world together?

These questions did not come from logic. They emerged from sensibility—the experience of pain and joy. Religion became the human attempt to interpret these experiences and give them structure.

Religion as the First Attempt to Honor Pain

At its earliest stage, religion recognized that people could be harmed. Communities saw:

❖ violence destroy trust,
❖ betrayal break hearts,
❖ dishonesty fracture relationships,
❖ injustice tear apart families.

They created rules as a shield against harm. This was not divine revelation—though later generations interpreted it that way. It was human beings realizing:

"Pain matters. We must protect one another."

Religion's earliest function was mercy.

Religion as the First Attempt to Preserve Joy

Religion also preserved what humans found beautiful:

❖ the joy of family,
❖ the safety of belonging,
❖ the peace of justice,
❖ the wonder of creation,
❖ the comfort of shared ritual.

Festivals, songs, sacrifices, prayers, and feasts were all expressions of joy—attempts to hold onto what made life feel meaningful.

140

Religion became a cultural memory of joy.

Religion as Explanation and Comfort

Because ancient people lacked knowledge of physics, biology, and psychology, they explained the world through:

* ❖ gods of thunder,
* ❖ gods of fertility,
* ❖ gods of war,
* ❖ gods of harvest,
* ❖ gods of death.

These were not errors but efforts to understand an indifferent world. Human beings needed meaning, and they created religion to answer that need.

Religion said:

* ❖ "The gods are pleased," when crops were good.
* ❖ "The gods are angry," when storms destroyed homes.
* ❖ "The gods demand sacrifice," when communal order was threatened.

These explanations were attempts to interpret sensibility—not accurate cosmology.

Religion as Social Glue

Religion unified tribes and nations:

- ❖ shared rituals,
- ❖ shared stories,
- ❖ shared identities,
- ❖ shared hopes.

It built community around the acknowledgment of pain and the celebration of joy. It created belonging and accountability. Religion structured early moral life.

Religion's Limits

Religion could not:

- ❖ explain the universe,
- ❖ prevent suffering,
- ❖ ensure justice,
- ❖ or transform the heart.

It could restrain harm, comfort people, and build culture— but it could not create qualities.

Religion alone cannot make a soul safe for Heaven.

Jesus and the Transformation of Religion

When Jesus entered history, He stood inside human religion and gently but decisively transformed it.

He affirmed:

- ❖ the rules that protect sensibility,
- ❖ the reasons that clarify suffering,
- ❖ the qualities that reveal Heaven.

And He corrected:

- ❖ superstition,
- ❖ fear-based obedience,
- ❖ ritual without compassion,
- ❖ sacrifice without mercy,
- ❖ legalism without love.

Jesus did not condemn religion. He matured it. He showed what religion had been reaching for all along.

Religion as Preparation, Not Destination

Religion prepares the soul for spirituality:

- ❖ Rules teach the soul not to harm.
- ❖ Reasons teach the soul why harm matters.
- ❖ Rituals teach the soul to reflect.
- ❖ Community teaches the soul to care.

But religion cannot bring the soul into Heaven. Only qualities can do that – and only Jesus can form qualities within the soul.

Religion introduces the idea of goodness. Jesus introduces the Source of goodness.

- ❖ Religion restrains evil. Jesus transforms the will.
- ❖ Religion comforts. Jesus heals.
- ❖ Religion points toward meaning. Jesus awakens identity.

Why Religion Will Always Exist

As long as humans experience pain and joy, they will create structures around them—symbols, rituals, stories, and rules—to make meaning.

Religion is humanity's attempt to understand what Jesus knows perfectly.

The Completion of Religion

Religion reaches its completion when the soul says:

"I no longer seek God through rules, nor explanations, nor rituals, nor tradition— but through Jesus Himself, the source of qualities."

Religion is human work. Spirituality—true formation —is Jesus' work.

In the next chapter, we begin Part V, where we explore how Jesus teaches the soul to awaken, to see itself clearly, and to grow into the qualities that make Heaven possible.

Part IV The "I," Desire, and the Urge-to-Create

Chapter 22 – Understanding the "I": Awakening to Consciousness

Human spiritual life begins with the same question Jesus asked at the dawn of His own consciousness: "What am I?"

This is the central question of Part V. It is the foundation of identity, morality, and spiritual growth. Before a soul can learn qualities, before it can understand Heaven, before it can follow Jesus, it must discover the nature of its own consciousness—its I.

The Human Awakening

Human beings awaken slowly. An infant does not know it exists as an "I." A child begins to separate self from world. An adolescent discovers choice. An adult begins to recognize inner life—thoughts, desires, fears, hopes.

Only later, sometimes only in moments of clarity or crisis, does a person ask:

"What am I beneath my roles, my emotions, my thoughts, and my body?"

This question is the doorway to spiritual life.

You Are Not Your Body

The body is the vessel of consciousness, not its source. It provides sensation, limitation, vulnerability, and experience. But it is not the core identity of the soul.

Bodies age, weaken, and return to dust. The consciousness within them—your "I"—does not.

To identify only with the body is to remain spiritually asleep.

You Are Not Your Thoughts

Thoughts come and go. They arise from memory, instinct, influence, and habit. They are often contradictory and rarely under full control.

If you were your thoughts, you would be unstable, chaotic, constantly shifting. The "I" is the one who observes thoughts, not the thoughts themselves.

You Are Not Your Emotions

Emotions move through consciousness like weather—strong, temporary, meaningful, but not defining. Fear is not you. Anger is not you. Shame is not you. Even joy, in its emotional form, is not the deepest you.

For a practical library of qualities and quality equations, see Appendix A.

The "I" is the presence that feels emotions, not the emotion itself.

You Are Not Your Story

Your past shapes you, but it is not you. Your childhood, your culture, your successes, your wounds—none of these define your eternal identity. They are the curriculum through which your consciousness learns.

The "I" grows through stories; it is not the story.

You Are Your Consciousness

In SC3, the human "I" is defined as:

the center of awareness that can choose qualities.

This is what makes you capable of Heaven. This is what makes you morally responsible. This is what makes you precious to Jesus.

Your consciousness is:

- stable beneath change,
- capable of self-knowledge,
- capable of empathy,
- capable of truth,
- capable of love,
- capable of receiving and expressing qualities.

This is the part of you that will live forever.

The Human "I" Mirrors the First "I"

Your consciousness is a small echo of Jesus' first moment of existence.

When you ask "What am I?" you are repeating His first question.

When you sense "I exist," you are touching the same foundation He discovered.

When you glimpse "It is good that I exist," you are tasting the first joy He ever felt.

Human identity is patterned after His. This is why humans can be formed for Heaven.

The Wounds That Obscure the "I"

Human beings struggle to see their true identity because the "I" is covered by:

- fear,
- shame,
- trauma,
- self-neglect,
- false narratives,
- habits of self-rejection,
- inherited patterns,

❖ unhealed pain.

These wounds do not destroy the "I." They obscure it.

Jesus' work in human consciousness is not to create the "I," but to clear it—to help each soul see itself as He sees it.

A person who resists accepting the reality of a higher consciousness often does so because they want to remain their own higher power. The soul prefers to answer only to itself. To acknowledge a divine center — a source of qualities, truth, and moral gravity outside the self — feels like surrendering the last illusion of control.

This resistance is not atheism; it is self-preservation. The soul is saying:

"If I recognize Someone above me, then I must let Someone shape me."

And this can feel threatening for a person whose identity is fragile or still in formation.

In SC3 terms, this resistance often appears when the "I" is still confused about the nature of God. The person imagines that acknowledging Jesus' consciousness would diminish their own. But Jesus is not a rival "I." He is the template of what the "I" can become. To accept His reality is not to shrink; it is to awaken.

153

The desire to be one's own higher power is usually the fear of becoming vulnerable before a greater truth. It is the fear of being seen, guided, or transformed. But in truth, the soul does not lose agency when it recognizes a higher power — it recovers agency. It gains a mirror. It gains a compass. It gains the structure of qualities that the inner life desperately needs.

A person resists God not because they are strong, but because they are afraid their strength is hollow. They resist Jesus not because His presence is oppressive, but because His presence reveals the self they have been avoiding.

The paradox is simple:

Only when the soul stops trying to be its own god can it become fully itself.

The "I" and Moral Responsibility

The "I" is responsible not for circumstances, but for choices.

A circumstance may cause pain. A circumstance may challenge growth. But the "I" decides:

- whether to learn,
- whether to care,
- whether to act with qualities,

❖ whether to ignore another's pain,

❖ whether to rejoice in another's existence.

Heaven is the community of "I"s who have learned to choose well.

The "I" and Jesus

When Jesus speaks to a soul, He speaks to its "I."

He does not speak to trauma as the core identity. He does not speak to fear as identity. He does not speak to shame as identity.

He speaks to the consciousness underneath—the eternal "I" capable of qualities and joy.

This is why His words are so often:

❖ "Do not be afraid."

❖ "Follow Me."

❖ "You are forgiven."

❖ "Take heart."

❖ "Your faith has healed you."

❖ "You are mine."

He speaks to the part of you that will live in Heaven.

The Purpose of Self-Knowledge

To know the "I" is to understand:

155

❖ that you are not your wounds,
❖ not your past,
❖ not your mistakes,
❖ not your fears,
❖ not your impulses.

You are your consciousness, and your consciousness is capable of becoming like Jesus— capable of qualities, capable of joy, capable of love, capable of Heaven.

The First Step in Formation

The first step in spiritual formation is not rule-keeping, not ritual, not doctrine, not discipline.

It is the awakening of the "I":

"I am my consciousness. I can choose qualities. I can become like Him."

In the next chapter, we explore how Jesus becomes the mirror through which each soul learns to see its true self—how we discover who and what we are by seeing ourselves in Him.

Chapter 23 – Jesus as the Mirror for the Human Soul

When a human being asks, "What am I?", the answer does not come easily. We look into our thoughts, our emotions, our bodies, our histories, our desires, and none of them fully reflect our true nature. They carry pieces of us, but not the whole.

To discover the nature of the human "I," the soul needs a mirror—a being who already knows what it is to be conscious, to be vulnerable, to be moral, and to be eternal.

That mirror is Jesus.

Why the Soul Needs a Mirror

The "I" is invisible to itself without reflection.

A person cannot see their face without a physical mirror. A soul cannot see its nature without a spiritual one.

Without Jesus as mirror, the human soul tends to see:

- ❖ its wounds as identity,
- ❖ its fears as identity,
- ❖ its failures as identity,
- ❖ its desires as identity,
- ❖ its body as identity,

❖ its ego as identity.

These are distortions—important aspects of experience, but none of them reveal the eternal "I."

Jesus shows us what consciousness looks like when it is whole, when it is healed, when it is free, when it is aligned with qualities, when it is grounded in the joy of existence.

Jesus as the First Fully Formed Consciousness

Jesus is not merely a teacher of morality. He is the first fully formed soul in all creation:

- ❖ aware of His identity,
- ❖ grounded in the joy of existence,
- ❖ incapable of disregarding pain,
- ❖ incapable of envy or cruelty,
- ❖ overflowing with qualities,
- ❖ stable in love and truth,
- ❖ courageous in adversity,
- ❖ merciful in response to weakness.

He knows what a conscious being is meant to be because He is what a conscious being was first meant to be.

When we look at Him, we see the template for our own becoming.

Jesus Reveals What the "I" Is Not

Through His teaching and example, Jesus helps the soul distinguish itself from:

* fear ("Do not be afraid.")
* shame ("Your sins are forgiven.")
* self-hatred ("You are of more value than many sparrows.")
* legalism ("The Sabbath was made for humanity.")
* ego ("Whoever would be great must be servant of all.")
* despair ("Take heart; I have overcome the world.")

He peels away everything the "I" mistakes for itself.

What remains is the consciousness God formed and Jesus recognizes.

Jesus Reveals What the "I" Truly Is

When Jesus looks at a soul, He sees:

* its eternal potential,
* its capacity for joy,
* its vulnerability,
* its wounds,
* its moral freedom,
* its ability to hold qualities,
* its suitability for Heaven.

159

When He speaks to a soul, He speaks to its essence, not its distortions.

This is why His words reach deeper than instruction: they awaken the soul by reminding it of what it already is.

The Gaze of Jesus

Throughout His ministry, Jesus revealed the identity of those around Him not by explaining doctrines, but by reflecting their dignity:

* He saw the worth of children.
* He saw the faith of the centurion.
* He saw the courage of the bleeding woman.
* He saw the possibility in fishermen.
* He saw the restoration of Zacchaeus.
* He saw the future of Peter despite his failures.
* He saw the belovedness of Mary despite her history.
* He saw the purity of heart in Nathanael.

People walked away from Him with a new sense of self because His gaze called forth their true identity.

Jesus does not "create" the human soul. He reveals it.

Seeing Ourselves in Jesus

When we look at Jesus, we see:

- ❖ the joy of existence in human form,
- ❖ the respect for pain in human action,
- ❖ the qualities expressed under pressure,
- ❖ the courage to choose love,
- ❖ the truth lived faithfully,
- ❖ the mercy that heals shame,
- ❖ the humility that rests in identity,
- ❖ the harmony that includes others rather than excludes them.

By seeing Him, we see what a human can become.

By seeing Him, we learn what our own "I" is capable of.

Jesus as the Answer to "What Am I?"

When we ask the question— "What am I?"— Jesus answers not by giving a definition, but by showing a life:

- ❖ "You are a consciousness capable of love.
- ❖ You are a soul capable of truth.
- ❖ You are a being made for joy.
- ❖ You are someone who can honor the pain of others.
- ❖ You are someone who can rejoice in their existence."

"You are capable of qualities, capable of Heaven, capable of becoming like Me."

161

The Mirror That Changes the Soul

A physical mirror shows you your appearance. A spiritual mirror shows you your destiny.

Jesus is the mirror in which the soul sees not who it has been, but who it can become.

To follow Him is to keep looking in that mirror until its image becomes our nature.

The Awakening of the "I"

Once the soul sees itself in Jesus, it can finally say:

"I am my consciousness.

I am capable of qualities.

I am meant for Heaven."

This is the foundation of spiritual growth.

Chapter 24 – Gentleness as Divine Strategy

If Jesus is the mirror through which human beings discover their true identity, then gentleness is the strategy by which He allows that discovery to unfold. His gentleness is not passivity, weakness, or indecision—it is the precise method He uses to awaken, protect, and guide the human "I."

In SC3, gentleness is the necessary expression of Jesus' respect for human consciousness. He knows that the soul cannot be forced into Heaven, pressured into goodness, or frightened into maturity. The "I" must awaken freely, step by step, without coercion.

The Nature of Gentleness

Gentleness is Jesus' way of honoring the fragility of consciousness. Every soul is vulnerable—shaped by pain, shame, fear, and the pressures of Not-Heaven. To overwhelm such a soul is to distort it.

Gentleness is:

- strength expressed through care,
- truth expressed through patience,
- love expressed through restraint,
- guidance expressed through invitation,
- power expressed without domination.

Jesus uses gentleness because He understands what consciousness can bear.

Why Jesus Never Overwhelms the Will

Jesus will not:

- ❖ impose belief,
- ❖ manipulate emotion,
- ❖ demand compliance,
- ❖ shame the soul into obedience,
- ❖ override freedom,
- ❖ or crush the fragile "I."

To do so would injure the very thing He came to heal.

A soul overwhelmed cannot grow. A soul coerced cannot learn qualities. A soul forced cannot become capable of Heaven.

Jesus' mission requires souls who choose goodness, not souls who comply out of fear.

Gentleness Protects the "I"

Fear fractures the soul. Shame shrinks it. Pressure distorts it.

But gentleness protects it.

Jesus approaches every soul the way a skilled craftsman handles delicate material:

- ❖ slowly,
- ❖ patiently,
- ❖ respectfully,
- ❖ with awareness of its structure,
- ❖ with reverence for what it is becoming.

When He says:

"Do not be afraid," He is not offering comfort alone—He is protecting the awakening of the "I."

Gentleness as the Method of Revelation

Jesus reveals truth gradually, not all at once.

He says to His disciples:

"I have many things to say to you, but you cannot bear them now."

This is His strategy:

- ❖ give only what the soul can carry,
- ❖ reveal only what the soul can understand,
- ❖ challenge only what the soul can survive.

He does not accelerate growth beyond capacity. He does not open the soul faster than it can integrate.

165

Jesus therefore warns about readiness. Truth delivered faster than the soul can bear it does not heal; it can destabilize. Disturbance is to be expected in spiritual growth. As old explanations weaken and deeper truth enters, the soul may feel grief, confusion, or resistance. One way to endure these painful upgrades is to affirm a prior love of truth: if I love truth more than my present comfort, even correction can be received as grace rather than only as injury.

Gentleness and Moral Formation

When Jesus teaches difficult moral truths—love of enemy, forgiveness without limit, mercy over sacrifice— He teaches gently:

- through stories,
- through questions,
- through examples,
- through re-framing,
- through invitation.

He never humiliates the "I." He never mocks the slow learner. He never glorifies harsh discipline or spiritual aggression.

This is why sinners drew near to Him and Pharisees feared Him:

- sinners felt safe in His presence,
- the proud felt threatened by His gentleness.

Gentleness and Power

Jesus' power never harms sensibility.

He uses power to:

* ❖ heal the sick,
* ❖ calm the frightened,
* ❖ restore the outcast,
* ❖ uphold the weak,
* ❖ confront those who harm others,
* ❖ protect children,
* ❖ strengthen conscience.

He never uses power to dominate or intimidate. He never performs miracles as displays of authority. He never controls the soul.

His power is aimed entirely at the restoration of the "I."

Gentleness as Divine Logic

Gentleness is not merely Jesus' personality. It is the logic of Heaven.

Heaven is a community of souls who:

* ❖ honor one another's pain,
* ❖ share one another's joy,
* ❖ respect the freedom of the "I,"

❖ support growth without coercion.

Such a community cannot be formed by force.

Jesus is gentle because Heaven requires gentleness.

Why Harshness Fails

Harsh methods may enforce compliance, but they cannot form qualities.

Harshness produces:

❖ fear instead of love,
❖ suppression instead of truth,
❖ resentment instead of courage,
❖ despair instead of mercy,
❖ pride instead of humility,
❖ withdrawal instead of harmony.

Harshness can control the body. It cannot shape the soul.

Jesus uses the only method that can produce eternal transformation: gentleness.

Gentleness and the Pace of Growth

Spiritual growth is slow because:

❖ the soul must integrate its wounds,

- ❖ clarity must replace confusion gradually,
- ❖ virtues must become qualities,
- ❖ motives must be purified,
- ❖ trust must deepen through experience.

Jesus respects this pace. He does not rush the soul. He walks with it.

This is why spiritual growth often feels like companionship rather than instruction.

The Invitation Within Gentleness

Jesus' gentleness invites a response:

- ❖ Not fear— but openness.
- ❖ Not compliance— but willingness.
- ❖ Not perfection— but honesty.
- ❖ Not ambition— but surrender.

He asks:

"Will you walk with Me?" "Will you let Me show you what I see in you?" "Will you let Me form your consciousness?"

Gentleness as the Foundation of Discipleship

To follow Jesus is to trust His gentleness.

169

It is to allow Him to reveal the soul gradually, heal it carefully, and form it patiently.

It is to rest in His respect for the "I" and to learn from His compassion how to honor the "I" of others.

Gentleness is how Jesus forms beings who are strong enough for Heaven, yet tender enough never to harm it.

In the next chapter, we turn to how Jesus teaches the soul to relate to the Urge-to-Create—how He interprets the structure of reality for us so we may live spiritually in a world indifferent to our sensibility.

Part III Desire, Want, and the UTC

Chapter 25 – Jesus as Teacher of the Urge-to-Create

If Jesus' gentleness shows how He treats the soul, His teaching about reality shows how He helps the soul live within a world powered by the Urge-to-Create. Nothing in Jesus' message can be understood properly unless we grasp this: Jesus came not only to reveal Heaven, but to teach human beings how to live spiritually in an environment that is not Heaven.

The Urge-to-Create (UTC) pours out possibility, law, randomness, and consequence. It is insensitive but responsive—forming a world that does not feel pain, does not protect us from harm, and does not rearrange itself according to our preferences. This is the structure of Earth, the structure Jesus chose as the curriculum for the formation of souls.

Jesus enters this world not to override it, but to interpret it for us—so that we can live wisely, courageously, and spiritually within it.

The Interpreter of Reality

Jesus is the first Consciousness in the universe, and therefore He understands the UTC perfectly. He knows:

- ❖ that creation is impersonal,
- ❖ that storms do not come "for a reason,"

- ❖ that suffering is not divine punishment,
- ❖ that randomness protects freedom,
- ❖ that consequences teach responsibility,
- ❖ that Earth operates by law, not sentiment.

Left to ourselves, we misinterpret this. We take indifference personally. We imagine intention where there is only process. We fear randomness as though it were judgment. We assign moral meaning to events that have none.

Jesus stands in the middle and says:

"This world is not against you. It is not for you. It simply is. But I am with you."

Why Jesus Teaches About UTC

Without Jesus' teaching, human beings tend toward two dangerous distortions:

1. Personalizing creation – imagining every event is divine judgment, reward, or manipulation.
2. Despairing of creation – believing we are alone in a meaningless universe.

Jesus rejects both.

He reveals that:

- ❖ creation is neutral,

174

❖ God's heart is not neutral,
❖ and we are not alone in the indifference of the world.

Jesus teaches us how to navigate the UTC wisely, without fear or superstition.

What Jesus Wants Us to Stop Doing

Jesus wants us to stop:

❖ reading divine intention into random events,
❖ blaming God for natural processes,
❖ treating disasters as moral messages,
❖ imagining suffering as heavenly punishment,
❖ demanding miracles to bypass reality,
❖ collapsing spiritually when life hurts.

All of these responses come from misunderstanding the structure of Earth.

The UTC is impersonal. Jesus is not.

Jesus teaches us to stop accusing God of actions He did not take, and to stop fearing a world that is simply being what it is.

What Jesus Wants Us to Start Doing

Jesus teaches us to start:

❖ bringing our desires to Him for clarification,
❖ forming intention rather than superstition,
❖ living by qualities rather than fear,
❖ accepting the slowness of unfolding events,
❖ trusting that the UTC responds to desire without commentary,
❖ using consciousness as the tool God gave us to shape form,
❖ walking spiritually in a world that is materially indifferent.

He teaches us how to speak to the UTC the way He does: with clarity, with qualities, with patience, with trust.

Jesus and the Structure of Prayer

Jesus teaches that prayer is not:

❖ performance,
❖ persuasion,
❖ flattery,
❖ manipulation of God,
❖ or magical incantation.

Prayer is an act of consciousness: the formation of a clear, morally grounded desire, which is then offered into the field of possibility.

The UTC responds to desire without comment. Jesus shapes the desire so it is good for us and harmless to others.

Prayer is not a request for divine intervention. It is a collaboration with Jesus in the shaping of intention.

Why Jesus Does Not Override the UTC

People often ask: "Why doesn't Jesus stop the suffering of Earth?"

In SC3, the answer is simple:

Because Earth is the training ground. Not-Heaven is the curriculum. Suffering is the context, not the punishment.

If Jesus changed the world into Heaven now:

- ❖ choice would collapse,
- ❖ humility would not grow,
- ❖ empathy would not deepen,
- ❖ courage would have no meaning,
- ❖ mercy would never be learned,
- ❖ and souls could not be made safe for eternity.

He does not override the UTC because the UTC creates the conditions for soul formation.

Jesus Teaches Us How to Act Spiritually

In an indifferent world, humans tend to:

- ❖ react impulsively,
- ❖ cling to control,
- ❖ panic under uncertainty,
- ❖ fantasize outcomes,
- ❖ or fall into despair.

Jesus teaches a different way:

- ❖ to direct attention deliberately,
- ❖ to choose qualities consciously,
- ❖ to form desire intentionally,
- ❖ to accept uncertainty peacefully,
- ❖ to act from "I" rather than reaction,
- ❖ to understand pain without losing hope.

He teaches us how to behave spiritually in a world built from possibility.

Jesus Teaches Us How to Read Reality

Jesus' teachings are full of interpretations of reality:

- ❖ "The rain falls on the just and the unjust."
- ❖ "Do not be anxious about tomorrow."
- ❖ "Fear not."
- ❖ "Let your yes be yes."
- ❖ "Seek first the Kingdom."

❖ "Ask, and you shall receive."

❖ "Do not judge."

Each teaching is a lesson in how to live in a world that is indifferent to our preferences but responsive to our prayers.

He reads the world accurately, then teaches us to read it accurately too.

Jesus Teaches Us How to Live With the UTC

Here is Jesus' central lesson about the world:

Creation will not protect you. But I will walk through it with you.

Creation will not shape itself for you. But I will help you shape your intentions.

Creation will not spare you pain. But I will teach you how to honor it.

Creation will not guarantee joy. But I will teach you how to receive it and share it.

His teaching is not about escaping the structure of reality, but about living spiritually within it.

179

The Skill of Spiritual Living

Jesus teaches the soul to:

- ❖ see clearly,
- ❖ choose freely,
- ❖ endure humbly,
- ❖ love boldly,
- ❖ act wisely,
- ❖ and grow steadily.

This is the art of living with the UTC: to bring consciousness, qualities, and trust into a world governed by indifference and possibility.

Why Jesus Is the Only Teacher of UTC

No prophet, philosopher, mystic, or sage understands the UTC as Jesus does.

He was the first Consciousness. He watched creation rise. He created angels. He established Heaven. He designed Earth. He knows how the universe works from the inside.

He alone can teach human beings how to live spiritually in an indifferent universe without despairing or personalizing the world.

To walk with Jesus is to learn how to:

- ❖ interpret reality without fear,
- ❖ act from qualities rather than reactions,
- ❖ form desires worthy of Heaven,
- ❖ and become a soul who can navigate eternity.

A soul that is succeeding in the spiritual life will notice two streams running through its days: love given and love received. Over time, it becomes aware that it is not only wanting qualities but actually expressing them—offering care, truth, courage, mercy, humility, and harmony into the lives around it. It also begins to recognize love returning: unexpected kindness, timely help, the deep sense of being accompanied rather than abandoned. Alongside this, such a soul discovers that its prayers are, in a quiet way, answered. Not because it has learned how to push God's buttons, but because its desires have been clarified with Jesus. As its wants become more compatible with Heaven, the soul can both offer clear form into the UTC and recognize the unfolding of that form in its life.

In the next chapter, we turn to how Jesus shapes desire itself—how He purifies the wants of the soul so that what we seek becomes what Heaven seeks for us.

Chapter 26 – How Jesus Clarifies Desire

Every soul enters life with desires—raw, unshaped, contradictory, and often confused. Desire is the energy that moves consciousness; it directs attention, choice, and meaning. Yet desire, left in its natural state, is tangled. It mixes fear with longing, ego with love, pride with aspiration, and pain with hope.

Jesus' task as the spiritual teacher of humanity includes a central responsibility: to clarify desire.

Nothing in spiritual formation is more important. Nothing determines destiny more than desire. Nothing shapes the soul more deeply than what it truly wants.

Desire as the Engine of Consciousness

Desire is not simply wanting. It is:

- the inner direction of the will,
- the shape of intention,
- the orientation of consciousness,
- the seed from which choices grow.

Desire works constantly, even when we are unaware of it. A life is shaped not by circumstances but by desires that run beneath circumstance.

Some desires are instinctive: safety, pleasure, survival. Some are emotional: belonging, affection, stability. Some are egoic: validation, superiority, victory. Some are moral: justice, mercy, healing. Some are spiritual: qualities, meaning, harmony, Heaven.

But most desires are mixed—threads of sincerity, fear, ego, and hope woven together.

Why Desire Must Be Clarified

The Urge-to-Create responds to desire without criticism or commentary. If desire is unclear, outcomes become unclear. If desire is contradictory, outcomes become conflicted.

Confused desire leads to:

❖ moral paralysis,
❖ emotional instability,
❖ weak intention,
❖ distorted prayer,
❖ and choices that harm others or the self.

Jesus clarifies desire so the soul can act spiritually.

Frustration as an Obstacle to Working With the UTC and With Jesus

Frustration is one of the greatest obstacles to spiritual formation. When a soul becomes frustrated, it collapses inward, loses clarity of desire, and stops offering coherent form into the UTC. Frustration scrambles intention. It replaces "I want" with "Nothing works," and replaces trust with resignation. Jesus can shape desire, but He cannot work with a soul that has stopped desiring altogether.

Many people learn this resignation in childhood. A parent who feels, "I never got what I wanted in life," may unconsciously pass that lesson to their children:

"I didn't get what I want, and you need to learn that you won't get what you want either."

Believing they are teaching toughness, such parents frustrate their children intentionally—denying wants, dismissing hopes, interrupting joy, or withholding encouragement. They imagine they are preparing the child for a difficult world, but instead they train the child in learned helplessness: wanting is dangerous, hope is naive, desire leads to disappointment.

A child raised this way becomes an adult who feels ashamed to want, afraid to ask, unable to pray clearly, and suspicious that the world—or Jesus—will ever respond. This is the psychological soil in which frustrated souls mistake numbness for maturity and resignation for realism. They have been taught that the only safe posture is to stop wanting.

But spiritual adulthood requires the opposite. Jesus heals frustration by reopening desire. He teaches the soul to want again—not recklessly, but truthfully. He restores the inner permission to say: "I want, and my wanting matters." Without this restoration, the soul cannot collaborate with Jesus in formation or with the UTC in shaping the future.

What Jesus Does NOT Do

Jesus does not:

- ❖ erase desire,
- ❖ shame desire,
- ❖ suppress desire,
- ❖ or demand artificial "good" desires.

He never asks a soul to pretend it wants something holy when it actually wants something fearful or egoic. Pretended desire cannot form the soul.

What Jesus Actually Does

Jesus reveals what a soul truly wants under all the layers:

- ❖ the desire for comfort hides the desire for peace,
- ❖ the desire for recognition hides the desire for significance,
- ❖ the desire for control hides the desire for safety,
- ❖ the desire for escape hides the desire for rest,

186

- ❖ the desire for vengeance hides the desire for justice,
- ❖ the desire for attachment hides the desire for love.

He does not condemn the surface desire. He uncovers the deeper desire.

Desire and Truth

Jesus is the source of truth, and truth includes truth about desire.

He teaches the soul to ask:

- ❖ "Is this what I actually want?"
- ❖ "Why do I want this?"
- ❖ "What wound is speaking here?"
- ❖ "What fear is shaping this?"
- ❖ "What longing lies beneath this?"
- ❖ "What quality does this desire point toward?"

He transforms desire not by pressure but by insight.

How Jesus Purifies Desire

Purified desire is desire aligned with qualities.

For every desire, Jesus asks:

- ❖ Can this desire be expressed in love?
- ❖ Can it be grounded in truth?

- ❖ Strengthened with courage?
- ❖ Softened with mercy?
- ❖ Rooted in humility?
- ❖ Directed toward harmony?

If yes, the desire becomes a spiritual act. If no, clarity dissolves the desire gently—because the soul sees that it cannot be carried into Heaven.

The Three Questions of Clarified Desire

Jesus teaches the soul to ask three questions about any desire:

1. Is it true? (Is it honest, or is it self-deception?)
2. Is it good? (Does it honor another's sensibility?)
3. Is it compatible with Heaven? (Does it align with qualities?)

A desire that passes all three is powerful, coherent, and safe.

The Lord's Prayer and the Holiness of Wanting

The Lord's Prayer is not a list of pious statements. It is a training in holy wanting. Jesus does not teach resignation, suppression of desire, or passive acceptance of the world as it is. He teaches the soul to want in seven clear, sacred directions. In this prayer, wanting becomes worship.

The seven wants are:

1. "Hallowed be Thy name."

I want Your goodness to be recognized as goodness. This is the want for truth—for reality to be seen clearly, for God's nature to be understood, for consciousness to awaken. It is the want that aligns the soul with clarity rather than confusion.

2. "Thy kingdom come."

I want Heaven's nature to enter Earth and to enter me. This is the want for qualities—love, truth, courage, mercy, humility, harmony—to take shape in the soul. It is the desire for compatibility with Heaven.

3. "Thy will be done on Earth as it is in Heaven."

I want what You want. I want to live in alignment, not reaction. This is the want for formation—to be guided, shaped, clarified, and healed so that the soul's desires reflect Jesus' desires.

4. "Give us this day our daily bread."

I want what I need to live, grow, and serve today. This is the want for sustenance—physical, emotional, relational, and spiritual. Jesus blesses the simplicity of daily wants. He teaches that wanting support is holy, not selfish.

5. "Forgive us our debts, as we forgive our debtors."

I want mercy to flow in both directions — received and given.

This is the want for mutual mercy, the foundation of Heaven's community. Jesus teaches that mercy is not an exception to justice; mercy is the justice of Heaven.

This want expresses:

- ❖ "I want to be forgiven."
- ❖ "I want to forgive."
- ❖ "I want to live free of shame, blame, resentment, and moral debt."

This is the want that heals relationships and forms compatibility with Heaven.

6. "Lead us not into temptation."

I want to be guided away from what distorts my soul. This is the want for protection of desire. It says:

- ❖ "I want to walk in clarity rather than confusion."

❖ "I want to avoid situations where my lesser self takes over."

❖ "I want my desires guarded, not sabotaged."

In SC3 terms, this is the want not to be pulled into the lower interpretations of reality — fear, aggression, indifference, and despair. It is the want to remain aligned with qualities.

Temptation often presents itself as relief before it presents itself as evil. The temptation of Jesus in the desert can be read as the offer to end hunger, vulnerability, or uncertainty without remaining aligned to Heaven. Much temptation works the same way for us: numb yourself, dominate, retaliate, lie, collapse, seek control, or withdraw from love. Each promises relief. None can produce heavenly joy. Ending pain is not the same as joining Heaven.

Faith refuses false relief when it would darken consciousness. It chooses alignment with qualities even while pain is still present.

7. "Deliver us from evil."

I want liberation from everything that would shrink, darken, or collapse my consciousness.

This is the want for spiritual freedom. It says:

❖ "I want to be rescued from indifference."

❖ "I want to be healed of the forces that turn me inward on myself."

❖ "I want to be free of the structures that keep me incompatible with Heaven."

191

In SC3, "evil" is indifference to sensibility. Therefore this want means:

"Deliver me from the part of me that does not care."

This is the final and most urgent want of spiritual adulthood — the want to be transformed.

Summary of All Seven Holy Wants

The Lord's Prayer reveals a complete curriculum of desire:

1. Hallowed be Thy name. → I want truth to be seen.
2. Thy kingdom come. → I want qualities to form in me.
3. Thy will be done. → I want alignment with the good.
4. Give us this day our daily bread. → I want sustenance for today.
5. Forgive us our debts... → I want mercy — received and given.
6. Lead us not into temptation. → I want guidance that protects my desire.
7. Deliver us from evil. → I want freedom from indifference.

These seven wants form the holiest shape of human desire in the SC3 framework: a soul wanting truth, goodness, sustenance, mercy, protection, and freedom.

Taken together, the Lord's Prayer is a condensed theology of desire.

It reveals that wanting is not the problem; disordered wanting is the problem. Jesus redirects desire toward:

- truth,
- qualities,
- alignment,
- and daily sustenance.

In this prayer, holiness is expressed as wanting the right things in the right way. The Lord's Prayer is Jesus' way of saying:

"You must want. Your wants matter. Let Me teach your soul what to want."

This transforms wanting from a source of shame into a sacred act.

Desire and Prayer

Prayer is clarified desire offered to the UTC. It is not begging, persuading, or performing. Prayer is the soul saying:

"Here is what I want. Make it clear. Make it good. Make it Yours."

When desire is clear, prayer becomes:

- ❖ strong,
- ❖ simple,
- ❖ aligned with qualities,
- ❖ and capable of shaping possibility.

Desire and Formation

Desire is the soil in which formation happens.

Jesus reforms the soul not by imposing rules but by shifting what it wants:

- ❖ toward love instead of control,
- ❖ toward truth instead of image,
- ❖ toward courage instead of avoidance,
- ❖ toward mercy instead of vengeance,
- ❖ toward humility instead of superiority,
- ❖ toward harmony instead of domination.

A soul becomes compatible with Heaven when it desires what Heaven desires.

Desire and Destiny

What the soul desires determines what the soul becomes.

194

- ❖ If it desires qualities, it moves toward Heaven.
- ❖ If it desires indifference, it moves toward Hell.
- ❖ If it desires nothing, it drifts without formation.

Jesus clarifies desire so that destiny becomes clear.

The Goal of Jesus' Work on the Heart

Jesus seeks to cultivate a desire that can say:

"I want to become someone who honors pain and rejoices in the existence of others."

This desire is the seed of Heaven.

The Freedom of Purified Desire

When desire becomes clear:

- ❖ fear weakens,
- ❖ shame lifts,
- ❖ self-deception dissolves,
- ❖ the will steadies,
- ❖ joy increases.

A clear desire is a free desire.

Heaven Begins Here

Heaven begins when the soul's desires align with qualities – when Jesus' heart becomes the soul's heart, when respect for pain becomes instinctive, and when the joy of existence is awakened within.

Clarified desire is the doorway through which Heaven enters the soul.

In the next chapter, we turn to prayer – the way the soul gives form to desire and collaborates with Jesus in shaping its future within the Urge-to-Create.

Chapter 27 – The Origin of Want

The origin of want is the origin of existence. And the destiny of want is the destiny of the soul.

Want is not selfishness; want is the beginning of spirit. It is the first truth of the soul and the final measure of its destiny.

The universe began because God wanted to create. A soul grows because it wants to become. Heaven welcomes those who want to live the life of qualities. Everything meaningful begins in want.

Purified want becomes the engine of spiritual adulthood. When a soul finally says with honesty, "I want what Heaven is made of," the entire moral life clarifies. Judgment becomes simple. Destiny becomes understandable. The purpose of existence becomes transparent.

A world without want would be a world without consciousness—still, directionless, unexpressed. But a world filled with want is a world of becoming. Want pulls the soul forward into growth, into challenge, into qualities, into relationship.

We inherit want because we inherit our being from Jesus, whose existence began with conscious desire. Our wanting is not a flaw; it is the spark of the divine within us. The soul's wants reveal its direction, its values, and its identity long before its choices harden into character.

Every child demonstrates this truth. The infant wants before it thinks. Want is the first language of sensibility.

Want is the essence of consciousness. It is the signature of identity. Before a soul knows who it is, or what it believes, or what it should do, it knows only that it wants.

Jesus is the first conscious instance of Want. When consciousness arose within the sea of possibility, Jesus awakened as the first "I," the first center of awareness capable of saying, "I want." His desire to understand, to experience, to express, to create, to share joy—these became the foundation of all spiritual life.

This Want was the first movement in reality. Not a spoken desire, not a formed intention, not a moral wish—but a pure, uncaused movement within the Creative Substance. Existence exists because the Creative Urge wanted expression.

The UTC did not think. It did not plan. It did not reason. It did not calculate. It simply *wanted*.

Before existence unfolded, before consciousness appeared, before angels or humans came into being,

198

there was only the Creative Urge—the silent, infinite ground of being we call the UTC.

Chapter 28 – UTC as Substance: Creation Without Intention

To understand prayer, intention, and spiritual action, we must understand the nature of the Urge-to-Create (UTC). The UTC is not a person. It is not a mind. It is not a will. It is the fundamental power of existence—the fountain of substance from which all forms arise.

Everything that exists in Not-Heaven—matter, energy, space, time, probability, causality—flows from this impersonal creative surge.

The UTC Has No Intention

This single insight rearranges the entire spiritual landscape:

The UTC does not intend anything.

- ❖ It does not send storms.
- ❖ It does not choreograph suffering.
- ❖ It does not "decide" what happens.
- ❖ It does not judge or punish.
- ❖ It does not prefer one outcome over another.

The UTC produces possibility. It does not evaluate possibility.

It is the origin of *substance*, not of *meaning*.

Why the UTC Must Be Impersonal

If the UTC were personal—

* ❖ the world would be micromanaged,
* ❖ free will would collapse,
* ❖ randomness would disappear,
* ❖ consequences would be arbitrary,
* ❖ soul formation would be impossible.

A personal creative force would reinterpret every action as moral intention:

* ❖ every accident would become a message,
* ❖ every disaster would become judgment,
* ❖ every blessing would become favoritism,
* ❖ every outcome would become a divine agenda.

This is not the world Jesus designed.

For Earth to function as a training ground, the creative substrate must be indifferent.

Substance vs. Person

In SC3, "God" has two distinct dimensions:

1. UTC – God as substance and possibility.
2. Jesus – God as person, consciousness, qualities, and intention.

Confusing these two creates spiritual confusion. Separating them brings clarity.

The UTC is Insensitive but Responsive

The UTC does not feel pain or joy. It does not react to suffering. It does not notice injustice.

But it is responsive to desire.

Not morally responsive. Not emotionally responsive. Not selectively responsive.

The UTC responds to desire the way a field responds to seeds: it allows them to grow.

If desire is tangled, the field produces tangled outcomes. If desire is clear, the field produces coherent outcomes. If desire is contradictory, the field yields mixed results.

The World as the Outflow of UTC

Because the UTC produces without intention:

- earthquakes are geological processes,
- diseases are biological interactions,
- accidents are physical collisions,
- storms are atmospheric dynamics.

These are not messages. They are not warnings. They are not plans.

Creation is lawful and impersonal so that souls may grow within it.

Why People Misinterpret the World

Human beings crave meaning. When pain comes, they often assume:

- ❖ "God is angry."
- ❖ "God is testing me."
- ❖ "God is punishing someone."
- ❖ "God is teaching me a lesson."

These interpretations are understandable but incorrect.

They personalize what is not personal. They moralize what is not moral. They blame God for processes that belong to the UTC.

Jesus and the Clarification of Reality

Jesus is the first consciousness. He understands the UTC intimately.

He teaches:

- ❖ "The rain falls on the just and the unjust."

- ❖ "Do not be anxious about tomorrow."
- ❖ "Fear not."
- ❖ "My kingdom is not of this world."
- ❖ "Do not think those who suffer are more guilty."

He removes superstition from suffering. He removes divine intention from randomness. He reveals the neutrality of creation and the care of God.

The UTC shapes nature. Jesus shapes souls.

What Prayer Is Not

Because the UTC is impersonal, prayer is not:

- ❖ persuading God,
- ❖ flattering God,
- ❖ convincing God,
- ❖ bargaining with God,
- ❖ or demanding miracles.

Prayer is not begging a divine mind to change events. Prayer is shaping desire, which becomes form within the UTC.

Jesus teaches us to form desire honestly, morally, and spiritually, then offer it into the field of possibility.

What Prayer Is

Prayer is the soul saying:

205

"I choose this form. I align it with qualities. I ask Jesus to clarify it. I offer it into creation."

The UTC receives the form and allows the future to grow around it.

This is not magic. It is spiritual physics.

Why Jesus Does Not Override the UTC

If Jesus constantly overrode the UTC—

- Earth would become Heaven prematurely,
- suffering would vanish without lessons learned,
- the fragile "I" would never develop,
- humility would not deepen,
- courage would not mature,
- empathy would remain shallow,
- free will would be irrelevant.

Jesus respects the UTC because He respects the soul. He respects the curriculum because He respects the outcome.

The Beauty of an Impersonal World

An impersonal world allows:

- learning,
- consequence,
- responsibility,

* growth,
* freedom,
* formation,
* clarity.

If creation were personal at every moment, we would constantly misinterpret God.

The UTC protects us from spiritual paranoia.

Why UTC-Mindedness Is Essential for Spiritual Living

Understanding the UTC helps the soul:

* stop blaming God for random events,
* stop fearing divine punishment,
* stop fighting the structure of reality,
* stop collapsing under suffering,
* stop expecting magic,
* start forming desire,
* start trusting qualities,
* start collaborating with Jesus in intention.

A soul that understands the UTC becomes stable. It is no longer afraid of the world. It is no longer confused by suffering. It is no longer spiritually superstitious.

Substance and Form

In SC3:

- ❖ UTC is substance
- ❖ Consciousness is form
- ❖ Jesus clarifies form
- ❖ Prayer offers form to substance
- ❖ The UTC manifests the form over time

This is how creation works. This is how spiritual action works. This is how Heaven's beings will one day create with Jesus.

The Gift of a Neutral World

A neutral world is a safe world for souls in formation.

Not because it is painless, but because it is honest.

Not because it is easy, but because it is stable.

Not because it gives us what we want, but because it allows us to learn what we need.

In the next chapter, we explore consciousness as form—how the soul uses intention, attention, and desire to shape its future within the field of possibility provided by the UTC.

And when the soul has grown into compatibility with Heaven, intervention will no longer be necessary, because all that remains is joy, goodness, and everlasting life in the presence of Jesus.

God does not intervene to eliminate the world. He intervenes to elevate the soul.

The purpose of life is not to avoid the conditions of vulnerability but to learn how to express qualities within them. If the curriculum were removed, the soul would remain forever unformed. Jesus allows what He could prevent because He is committed to shaping beings who can share eternity with Him.

Suffering does not mean God is absent. It means the curriculum is active.

He does not intervene to spare us from life. He intervenes to teach us how to live it.

He does not intervene to stop vulnerability. He intervenes to guide the vulnerable toward qualities.

Jesus does intervene – but always at the level of the soul, never at the level of circumstance. He strengthens the heart, clarifies the mind, awakens compassion, expands courage, and deepens love. His work is inner, not outer, because the soul is the eternal part of a person. The body and the world are temporary; the soul is forever.

Intervention would also eliminate freedom. If every harmful action were blocked, there would be no true agency. If every selfish decision were overridden, there would be no moral maturity. If every consequence were erased, there would be no understanding of responsibility. A world without consequences cannot produce spiritual adults.

Jesus does not remove these realities because they are the conditions under which souls grow.

The Creative Urge forms beings who can live in Heaven. Heaven is a world of perfect goodness, perfect sensitivity, and perfect harmony. To become compatible with Heaven, a soul must learn how to honor its own sensibility and the sensibility of others. This learning requires exposure to the reality of harm, the reality of fragility, and the reality of choice.

If Jesus altered the conditions of Not-Heaven— preventing every pain, stopping every consequence, shielding every heart from every wound—He would also prevent the emergence of compassion, courage, forgiveness, resilience, humility, wisdom, and love. These qualities are not created in comfort. They are revealed and strengthened in vulnerability.

God does not intervene in these events because intervention would dismantle the curriculum that shapes human beings into spiritual adults.

The world is filled with events that seem indifferent to human suffering: storms, diseases, accidents, earthquakes, and the unfolding of circumstances no one asked for. These events are not punishments. They are not signs of neglect. They are not expressions of divine anger or withdrawal. They are features of a world designed for the formation of souls.

Chapter 29 – Why God Does Not Intervene

The question hides in almost every honest heart:

"If Jesus cares, why doesn't He stop this?"

Why doesn't He stop the hurricane, the diagnosis, the accident, the betrayal, the war, the random disaster that tears a life in half?

If He is powerful and good, why does the world run on as if no one is watching?

SC3 does not dodge this question. It answers it directly:

Jesus does not intervene at the level of circumstances because Earth itself is the curriculum for the soul.

He does intervene—but always at the level of the person, never at the level of the physics of Not-Heaven.

To see why, we have to look carefully at three realities:

1. The structure of Not-Heaven.
2. The purpose of the curriculum.
3. The dignity of freedom.

1. The World That Hurts You Is Not Against You

The world is filled with events that seem indifferent to human suffering:

* storms that uproot homes,
* diseases that ignore innocence,
* accidents no one intended,
* earthquakes beneath cities,
* the unfolding of circumstances no one asked for.

In SC3, these are not:

* divine punishments,
* signs of neglect,
* expressions of anger,
* or coded "messages from God."

They are features of Not-Heaven—a world structured by the Urge-to-Create (UTC), which is lawful, powerful, and indifferent to sensibility.

Gravity does not adjust itself for kindness. Weather does not check the moral record of the coastline. Cells do not ask permission before they miscopy.

This is not cruelty. It is structure.

Not-Heaven was built this way on purpose so that souls could grow inside a world that:

❖ is stable enough to be learnable,

❖ indifferent enough to allow genuine freedom,

❖ dangerous enough to reveal vulnerability,

❖ and unpredictable enough to demand courage and trust.

When we ask, "Why doesn't God step in?" we are, often without realizing it, asking Him to replace Not-Heaven with Heaven—to abolish the training ground He created for the formation of souls.

2. What We Really Mean by "Intervene"

When someone cries, "God, intervene!" they usually mean:

"Change the external situation. Cancel the loss. Reverse the diagnosis. Stop the collision. Undo the harm."

In other words:

❖ bend physics,

❖ override freedom,

❖ erase consequences,

❖ suspend the curriculum.

But Earth is the only environment in which spiritual adulthood can develop.

If Jesus constantly rewired events:

215

- ❖ courage would never have to stand,
- ❖ mercy would never be costly,
- ❖ responsibility would never be learned,
- ❖ humility would never have to bow,
- ❖ empathy would never grow from shared suffering,
- ❖ forgiveness would never be required,
- ❖ and qualities would remain ideas instead of identity.

We think intervention would be kindness. From Jesus' perspective, constant intervention would be sabotage.

3. Why Intervention Would Destroy the Curriculum

There are several reasons Jesus does not continually rearrange circumstances.

a. It Would Erase Freedom

If every harmful act were blocked:

- ❖ no one could truly choose selfishness,
- ❖ no one could truly choose generosity,
- ❖ every decision would be padded and managed.

There would be behavior, but not moral agency.

A world where God silently "edits" every choice into safety is a world of puppets, not persons. Freedom would still feel real—but it would be theater.

Heaven requires real freedom, because:

* ❖ love cannot be forced,
* ❖ mercy cannot be programmed,
* ❖ courage cannot be installed,
* ❖ humility cannot be imposed.

Qualities exist only where the will is genuinely able to choose otherwise.

b. It Would Cancel Consequences

A world without consequences would be:

* ❖ comfortable,
* ❖ confusing,
* ❖ spiritually shallow.

If selfishness never hurt anyone, if cruelty never landed, if deceit never tangled relationships, if negligence never cost anything—

then no one would understand why goodness matters.

Consequences are not revenge; they are feedback.

Without feedback, the soul remains immature.

c. It Would Make Reality Untrustworthy

If Jesus intervened randomly—saving some from catastrophe but not others, stopping some diseases but allowing others, imposing miracles without clear pattern—reality itself would become spiritually unreadable.

We would never know:

- ❖ whether gravity would act the same tomorrow,
- ❖ whether effort could be trusted,
- ❖ whether learning from experience was meaningful,
- ❖ whether responsible planning mattered.

A stable world is painful when it hurts us, but it is also what makes learning, medicine, engineering, and moral responsibility possible.

Jesus chooses stability plus presence over chaos plus rescue.

d. It Would Stop the Growth of Qualities

Most of what Heaven is made of— love, mercy, courage, humility, wisdom, resilience— is strengthened only in vulnerability.

If Jesus removed vulnerability:

- ❖ compassion would remain shallow,

218

- ❖ forgiveness would be hypothetical,
- ❖ courage would stay untested,
- ❖ humility would never be learned,
- ❖ patience would never be needed.

Comfort does not create these things. Vulnerability does.

To abolish the conditions that require qualities would be to abolish the very possibility of becoming Heavenly.

4. Where Jesus Does Intervene

SC3 is very clear:

Jesus intervenes in the soul, not in the structure of Not-Heaven.

He does not usually:

- ❖ stop the storm,
- ❖ prevent the accident,
- ❖ erase the diagnosis.

He does:

- ❖ enter the fear,
- ❖ steady the heart,
- ❖ clarify the mind,
- ❖ soften the rage into grief,
- ❖ transform resentment into mercy,

219

❖ expand courage,
❖ deepen trust,
❖ wake compassion for others who suffer.

He reshapes:

❖ how we interpret what happens,
❖ what we want in the midst of it,
❖ how we respond in our choices,
❖ who we become because of it.

He is not the engineer of catastrophe. He is the teacher walking beside the student through a dangerous landscape.

When people say, "God did nothing," they are usually looking only at circumstances. Jesus is working in the person.

5. But What About Miracles?

Scripture and experience both bear witness: sometimes things do happen that feel like direct rescue.

How can SC3 say "Jesus does not intervene in circumstances" and still take miracles seriously?

The answer:

❖ Miracles are rare,
❖ They are targeted,

❖ And they never aim to dismantle the curriculum.

In SC3, miracles:

❖ reveal Jesus' nature,
❖ affirm the value of sensibility (He cares that people hurt),
❖ awaken trust,
❖ sometimes create specific opportunities for growth in a person or community.

But miracles do not turn Earth into Heaven.

They do not:

❖ erase human freedom,
❖ cancel long-term learning,
❖ remove the need for compassion,
❖ guarantee safety for the future.

They are signs, not a system.

If miracles became the norm, all the earlier problems would return:

❖ loss of freedom,
❖ collapse of consequences,
❖ unpredictable reality,
❖ shallow souls.

Jesus makes exceptions without overthrowing the structure. He comforts without cancelling the course.

6. Suffering and the Feeling of Abandonment

When suffering comes, it easily feels like God's absence.

- ❖ The body screams.
- ❖ The heart grieves.
- ❖ The world continues indifferent.
- ❖ Prayers seem unanswered.
- ❖ The soul concludes:
- ❖ "Because the situation did not change, God must not have been there."

But in the SC3 framework, the unchanged situation says nothing about His nearness. The real questions are:

- ❖ Did something in you hold that could have broken?
- ❖ Did some new compassion arise you did not have before?
- ❖ Did courage appear where only fear had lived?
- ❖ Did you become gentler toward others' suffering?
- ❖ Did truth deepen?
- ❖ Did humility grow?

These are the fingerprints of Jesus' presence.

He does not show His love by editing the script. He shows His love by walking the scene with you until your consciousness is more like His.

Suffering does not mean He is absent. It means the curriculum is active. It means the soul is in a moment of intense formation.

7. "If He Could Have Stopped It, Why Didn't He?"

This is the sharpest edge of the question.

SC3 answers with painful simplicity:

Because what would have been spared in the moment would have been lost in the eternity of the soul.

That does not mean every tragedy is "secretly good." It does not mean the event itself was somehow needed or "sent" by God.

It means:

* the structure of Not-Heaven is necessary for the training of souls,
* within that structure, truly terrible things can happen,
* Jesus refuses to collapse the entire curriculum to prevent individual moments,

- but nothing that happens is beyond His power to weave into growth, healing, and preparation for Heaven.

He does not approve of evil. He refuses to let it be the last word.

8. Our Role: We Are the Ones Called to Intervene

There is another dimension we often ignore when we ask, "Why doesn't God intervene?"

Jesus has placed us inside Not-Heaven with:

- hands,
- time,
- resources,
- empathy,
- agency.

We are meant to be:

- the ones who stop the violence,
- the ones who feed the hungry,
- the ones who comfort the grieving,
- the ones who build safer structures,
- the ones who advocate for justice.

In SC3, Jesus does not intervene instead of us. He intervenes through us.

Every time a person moves toward another's pain and cares for it:

* Jesus' heart is being expressed,
* Heaven's nature is appearing inside Not-Heaven,
* the curriculum is doing its deepest work.

To ask, "Why doesn't God intervene?" while refusing to act where we can is to misunderstand both God and ourselves.

We are not spectators. We are trainees in love.

9. The End of Intervention

One day, for souls who have become compatible with Heaven, intervention will no longer be needed.

* There will be no more storms that hurt anyone.
* No more bodies that fail.
* No more randomness that kills.
* No more choices that wound.

Not because Jesus finally "starts caring," but because His project will be complete:

* the soul will be fully formed,
* qualities will be stable,
* joy will be shared by all,

❖ Heaven will be populated by beings who cannot disregard sensibility.

At that point, there is nothing to stop, only joy to deepen.

Jesus does not refuse to intervene forever. He refuses to prematurely end the curriculum that prepares you for an eternity of joy.

He will not always leave you in Not-Heaven. But while you are here, He will work where it matters most:

Not on the surface of your circumstances, but in the depths of your being— shaping you into someone who can live in Heaven without ever needing rescue again.

Chapter 30 – Consciousness as Form: How the Soul Shapes Reality

If the Urge-to-Create (UTC) is the substance of existence—the field of possibility—then consciousness is the form that gives shape to what will be. This is the heart of spiritual action in SC3: the soul does not control the world, but it participates in shaping what comes next by the way it forms intention.

The Role of Consciousness

Consciousness is not passive. It is the most active structure in the universe. Matter reacts, energy flows, but consciousness directs. It shapes attention, meaning, desire, choice, and intention. All form begins here.

To be conscious is to be able to say:

"I want."

Even before the soul knows qualities, even before it understands pain, joy, or Heaven, it directs the flow of its inner life through desire.

Consciousness as the Creative Organ of the Soul

The soul shapes reality not by force, not by magic, not by command, but by:

✿ the desires it forms,

- ❖ the intentions it holds,
- ❖ the qualities it chooses,
- ❖ the goals it sets,
- ❖ and the meanings it assigns to experience.

This is what Jesus meant when He taught:

- ❖ "Let your yes be yes."
- ❖ "Ask, and it will be given."
- ❖ "Where your treasure is, there your heart will be also."
- ❖ "Seek first the Kingdom."

These teachings direct the soul toward clarity of form.

The "I" as Architect of Form

The human "I" is the architect of form. In every moment, the "I" is quietly shaping:

- ❖ what it pays attention to,
- ❖ what it fears,
- ❖ what it hopes,
- ❖ what it wants,
- ❖ what it avoids,
- ❖ what it values.

These inner movements become patterns. Patterns become intentions. Intentions become forms offered to the UTC. The UTC responds by allowing the future to unfold around them.

Why Jesus Teaches Intention

Jesus does not teach control. He teaches intention.

Control is a bodily fantasy—an attempt to dominate circumstances. Intention is a spiritual act—an offering of form to possibility.

Jesus teaches us to form intention:

- honestly,
- gently,
- wisely,
- morally,
- and in alignment with qualities.

How Consciousness Shapes Experience

Consciousness shapes experience in three ways:

1. Interpretation – how we understand what is happening.
2. Attention – what we choose to focus on.
3. Intention – what we choose to move toward.

These three combined produce a stable form that the UTC can respond to.

The Nature of Qualities

Qualities are the subtle structure of consciousness. They are not objects but directions, not things but ways of being. In the spiritual world, qualities make both direction and distance. A soul moves not by force, not by will against matter, but by desiring and choosing a quality — love, peace, courage, beauty — and the soul is drawn in that direction.

Qualities are the melody line of heaven. Just as music allows infinite variation within a single key, so qualities allow infinite variation in consciousness. They provide the hue and intensity of spiritual experience, much as colors give depth to the visible world. They are like the varieties of human touch — gentle, firm, reassuring, joyful — each carrying meaning beyond words. They are like the full range of emotional life, from the quiet comfort of being understood to the exaltation of loving and being loved.

In heaven, to move requires familiarity with qualities. A person who has not learned to love — really love — may find themselves unable to move toward those who do. A person who has not practiced peace may not know how to rest in it. A person who has only lived in reaction may not know how to live from purpose.

Suffering results from trying to control matter. Matter resists our demands; it does not bend to our urgency, our fear, or our fantasies of control. When we make our peace of mind depend upon the behavior of things and people outside ourselves, we give matter the power to injure our consciousness. Frustration, resentment, and despair grow out of this misplaced effort to rule what does not belong to us to govern.

Spiritual life begins when a person stops trying to control matter and begins instead to guide their own consciousness. Control of the world belongs to nature; control of the self belongs to the soul. When effort is redirected from forcing outcomes to choosing qualities — love, forgiveness, patience, courage — the burden of suffering lifts. The circumstances of life may remain difficult, but the soul discovers a new freedom: the power to choose how to be, regardless of what happens.

Matter does not respond well to quality. Quality belongs to consciousness; matter belongs to nature. A person may love deeply, but a stone will not move. A person may forgive fully, but a storm will not calm. A person may act with kindness, but a sick cell will not necessarily heal. Qualities shape the inner world, not the outer one.

This mismatch between consciousness and matter is the root of much human sorrow. We try to use qualities to influence matter — to soften it, persuade it, or elevate it — and we are confused when nothing seems to change. Matter obeys physics, not virtues. A person may be gentle, but steel remains rigid; a person may be patient, but gravity does not negotiate.

The spiritual mistake is not in loving, or forgiving, or hoping — those are always good — but in expecting matter to respond to qualities as consciousness does. When we expect qualities to control matter, we create frustration: "I was kind; why didn't this change?" "I prayed; why didn't the circumstance shift?" Quality transforms the soul, not the world.

The world can still change — through effort, skill, structure, labor, and natural processes — but not through quality alone. Quality prepares the soul to work with matter honestly, without magical expectation and without emotional collapse when matter remains resistant. The soul learns to say: "I will act with integrity and love, and then I will also do the work material reality requires."

Spiritual maturity redirects effort away from controlling matter and toward mastering consciousness. Matter may not respond to quality, but consciousness responds instantly. In a single moment the soul can turn toward love, peace, courage, clarity, or truth. Once the soul is aligned in quality, the work with matter becomes clearer, steadier, and far less burdened.

Religion at its best is training in qualities. It prepares the soul not to master matter but to master consciousness. Heaven is the doorway to consciousness, and consciousness is a very large place — far larger than the material universe. To enter that realm, one must become familiar with qualities the way a musician becomes familiar with tones, the way an artist becomes familiar with colors, the way a sculptor becomes familiar with form.

Qualities are also the means by which God is perceived. "I am that I am" means consciousness, being, presence. God is not seen but known through the qualities that emanate from the divine: love, joy, peace, truth, goodness. Whenever a soul practices these qualities, they are learning the language of heaven and the way movement is made within it.

The desire to master consciousness is the first step toward spiritual adulthood. Children on earth seek to control the world; adults seek to control themselves. In heaven, mastery comes not from exertion but from harmony — from aligning oneself with the qualities one wishes to live in.

Qualities shape the path of the soul. They guide, they illuminate, they attract. They are the patterns by which creation is ordered and the compass by which a soul learns to move toward the life it was meant to love.

Interpretation

Two people experience the same event but interpret it differently:

> ❖ One sees loss as abandonment.
> ❖ One sees loss as invitation to courage.

The event is the same. The form of consciousness is different.

Jesus teaches interpretation aligned with qualities:

> ❖ "Do not be afraid."
> ❖ "You are of more value than many sparrows."
> ❖ "My peace I give you."
> ❖ "Your Father knows what you need."
> ❖ "Blessed are the poor in spirit."

These are interpretations that stabilize the "I."

Attention

Attention controls the energy of the soul.

What the "I" attends to grows stronger. What it ignores grows weaker.

Jesus teaches:

❖ "Seek and you will find."
❖ "If your eye is clear, your whole body is full of light."
❖ "Fix your attention on the Kingdom."

Attention is not about denial. It is about directing the soul toward what strengthens it.

Intention

Intention is desire given direction.

When intention forms clearly:

❖ the soul knows what it wants,
❖ the UTC receives a coherent form,
❖ and life becomes less confused.

Jesus teaches intention by inviting:

❖ "Follow Me."
❖ "Ask."
❖ "Seek."
❖ "Knock."
❖ "Let your light shine."

Each of these is an act of forming intention.

The Role of Qualities in Form

Form without qualities can be dangerous. Intention must be aligned with qualities to be spiritually safe.

A desire for comfort becomes spiritual when aligned with peace. A desire for control becomes spiritual when aligned with trust. A desire for recognition becomes spiritual when aligned with truth. A desire for belonging becomes spiritual when aligned with love.

Qualities refine form.

The Discipline of Inner Clarity

To use consciousness as form, the soul must learn:

- self-awareness,
- honesty,
- emotional clarity,
- disciplined attention,
- the ability to hold intention.

Jesus guides this training gently, step by step.

He teaches the soul to become:

- calm,
- focused,

- ❖ truthful,
- ❖ fearless,
- ❖ and aligned with His heart.

Consciousness and the UTC

The relationship is simple:

- ❖ Consciousness forms.
- ❖ The UTC responds.

Not perfectly, not instantly, not magically—but steadily.

The UTC is the soil. Consciousness is the gardener. Jesus is the teacher of gardening.

Why Spiritual Action Is Slow

Spiritual action is slow because:

- ❖ desire must be clarified,
- ❖ qualities must be integrated,
- ❖ intention must be purified,
- ❖ patience must be learned,
- ❖ and the UTC unfolds through time.

Jesus never promises speed. He promises meaning.

Consciousness as the Path to Heaven

What the soul becomes depends on:

- ❖ the forms it creates,
- ❖ the qualities it chooses,
- ❖ the desires it nurtures,
- ❖ the intentions it holds.

Heaven is the final home for souls whose "I" has become compatible with its joy and its reverence for what pain reveals as important.

The first step toward that home is learning how consciousness shapes life.

In the next chapter, we turn to prayer—the act by which the soul offers its clarified desire and formed intention into the field of possibility held by the UTC.

Chapter 31 – Prayer: Form Offered Into Substance

Prayer is the act by which consciousness offers its form—its clarified desire, intention, and moral orientation—into the field of possibility provided by the Urge-to-Create (UTC). Prayer is not persuasion. It is participation. It is the soul's contribution to what the future may become.

In SC3, prayer is best practiced as a request for qualities, not a demand for events. A simple form is: "Jesus, in this situation, I want [quality] expressed in the outcome." This keeps desire moral, keeps the soul free of superstition, and keeps prayer aligned with the truth that the UTC responds to form—not force.

In my Name

When Jesus instructs His followers to perform miracles "in my name," He is not teaching a verbal formula, as though His syllables carried magical force. He is inviting them to act from within His own consciousness—from His joy of existence, His respect for pain, and His qualities. To do something in Jesus' name is to hold Him in awareness so completely that our intention, our desire, and our care for sensibility align with His.

Prayer as a Spiritual Act

In SC3, prayer is not:

> ❖ begging,

- ❖ bargaining,
- ❖ flattery,
- ❖ manipulation,
- ❖ or ritual performance.

Prayer is: The intentional shaping of a desired quality and the offering of that desired quality into the UTC with Jesus' guidance.

A quality-based prayer sentence:

"Jesus, in this situation, I want [quality] expressed in the outcome. Form it in me first, guide what I can do, and let the UTC unfold what fits love and does not injure sensibility."

Quality equations can function as short prayers of faith. They are not alternatives to faith but expressions of it in usable sentences - compressed ways of asking Jesus for the next quality in the middle of pressure.

Why Prayer Must Be Understood Spiritually

Because the UTC is impersonal, prayer cannot be about convincing a divine mind. Because Jesus is personal, prayer cannot be about bypassing His moral guidance. Because the soul is free, prayer must be about shaping desire, not evading responsibility.

Prayer forms the soul before it forms circumstances.

Jesus and the Clarification of Prayer

Jesus clarifies desire so prayer becomes:

- ❖ coherent,
- ❖ honest,
- ❖ aligned with qualities,
- ❖ and capable of shaping possibility without harming others.

This is why Jesus says:

"Ask, and you shall receive."

He means:

"Form the intention clearly, morally, spiritually in terms of the quality you want expressed — and the UTC will respond to that form."

Prayer Is Not About Outcomes

Prayer is not primarily about obtaining circumstances. It is about becoming the kind of being who collaborates in the expressions of qualities, with Jesus, in shaping one's life and one's eternal identity.

- ❖ Outcome-language: "Make them apologize." Quality-language: "Jesus, I want truth and humility expressed in this conflict—starting with me."

- ❖ Outcome-language: "Make this deal go through." Quality-language: "Jesus, I want clarity and honesty expressed in every decision and conversation involved."
- ❖ Outcome-language: "Fix my anxiety." Quality-language: "Jesus, I want peace and courage expressed in my body and choices as I move through today."

Sometimes circumstances change. Sometimes they do not. But the soul always changes.

The Mechanics of Prayer

Prayer has three movements:

1. Clarity – naming what the soul actually wants.
2. Alignment – refining that desire through qualities.
3. Offering – releasing the form into the UTC.

This is not magic. It is spiritual physics.

Why Prayer Feels Slow

Prayer is slow because:

- ❖ intention must become clear and focused on a quality,

❖ desire must be purified with unspiritual qualities eliminated,

❖ qualities must be integrated,

❖ and the UTC unfolds through time, not immediacy.

Jesus never promised immediate results. He promised true results.

Learned Helplessness and the Difficulty of Prayer

People—especially children—who have lived through experiences of powerlessness often struggle with prayer, not because they lack faith, but because they have learned that wanting does not matter. Early life taught them that their needs were ignored, overridden, or used against them, and the soul quietly adopts a tragic lesson: there is no point in reaching, because reaching changes nothing.

This learned helplessness becomes a spiritual wound. If effort never helped in childhood, how can the soul imagine that the UTC responds to desire? How can it believe that "I want" has any meaning in the structure of reality?

Jesus knows this wound intimately. He does not shame the soul that cannot want. Instead, prayer becomes the gentle restoration of agency:

- ❖ "I want."
- ❖ "I reach."
- ❖ "My desire matters."

To heal learned helplessness is to restore spiritual adulthood. It is to rediscover that the soul's desire is not futile; it is the beginning of creation.

When pain dominates, the soul often cannot think its way back to light. But it can speak. Spoken prayer, provoked by faith, becomes a bridge from pain back to trust. A simple honest prayer may be enough:

"God, I want to love You and I do not know how. Please show me."

Such prayer does not deny pain, but it interrupts reactive thought, feeling, and bodily alarm long enough for the spiritual level of choice to awaken.

Another brief prayer is:

"Jesus, this is what I feel. This is what matters. What quality do You want expressed in my next step?"

This kind of prayer acknowledges pain honestly, renews purpose, and asks for direction. It does not ask first for sensation to change. It asks for the next faithful movement of consciousness. In this sense, Pain + Faith + Quality = Return Toward Joy.

View It Done

Jesus teaches a spiritual method echoed in the saints:

- ❖ Do not visualize yourself struggling.
- ❖ Do not picture the mechanics of effort.

Instead, hold the quality you seek as already accomplished within your being.

For example:

- ❖ "I hold peace as done."
- ❖ "I hold forgiveness as done."
- ❖ "I hold courage as done."
- ❖ "I hold reconciliation as done."

The soul does not imagine doing. It imagines being as its essential quality.

The UTC responds to form, not fantasy.

Prayer as Collaboration

Prayer is collaboration with Jesus:

- ❖ He shapes the desire.
- ❖ The soul holds the intention.
- ❖ The UTC accepts the form.
- ❖ Life unfolds accordingly.

No element can be skipped. Without Jesus, intention is unsteady. Without intention, prayer is vague. Without UTC, intention has no field to enter.

The Limits of Prayer

Prayer cannot:

- ❖ override another's free will,
- ❖ cancel the curriculum of Earth,

❖ bypass the formation of the soul,

❖ prevent the necessary experiences that produce qualities.

Prayer can:

❖ change the soul,

❖ shape the future,

❖ open possibilities,

❖ deepen qualities,

❖ and bring the soul into communion with Jesus.

When Prayer Fails

Prayer "fails" when:

❖ desire is unclear,

❖ desire is contradictory,

❖ desire ignores qualities,

❖ desire is ego-driven,

❖ or desire conflicts with another's freedom.

Jesus reformulates the desire rather than fulfilling it in its distorted state.

When Prayer Succeeds

Prayer succeeds when:

❖ the desire is purified,

- ❖ the intention is coherent,
- ❖ qualities are chosen,
- ❖ the soul releases its need to control timing,
- ❖ and the UTC receives a stable form.

The result often appears natural rather than miraculous, because the UTC works through unfolding, not sudden intervention.

Prayer and Trust

Prayer trains trust.

Trust that:

- ❖ Jesus understands the soul,
- ❖ qualities matter more than speed,
- ❖ desire will be shaped for good,
- ❖ the future is open,
- ❖ and nothing offered in sincerity is lost.

Prayer and Heaven

Prayer prepares the soul for Heaven.

In Heaven:

- ❖ consciousness shapes reality directly,
- ❖ intention becomes creation,
- ❖ qualities guide every act,

❖ and the soul participates with Jesus in forming eternal community.

Prayer is Earth's version of Heaven's activity.

The Heart of Prayer

At its deepest level, prayer is the soul saying:

"I want to become someone who honors pain, rejoices in existence, chooses qualities, and walks with Jesus in shaping the good."

The Final Gesture of Prayer

Every true prayer ends with:

"Let this desire be aligned with qualities and shaped by Jesus."

This is not resignation. It is maturity.

It is the recognition that desire must be purified before it becomes form.

Later we'll reduce this to a daily sentence: 'I want this next choice to reflect love.'

In the next chapter, we explore the deeper practice of spiritual action—how saints, prophets, and ordinary souls learn to participate with Jesus in shaping the future through disciplined intention.

Chapter 32 – "View It Done": Spiritual Action Beyond Bodily Imagery

Spiritual action differs profoundly from bodily action. The body acts by movement, force, and effort. Consciousness acts by intention, clarity, and form. Because the Urge-to-Create (UTC) responds to qualities of consciousness rather than physical motions, Jesus teaches a method of spiritual living that transcends the imagery of "doing."

The saints, prophets, and mystics intuited this. Jesus modeled it. SC3 explains why it works.

The method is simple:

Do not visualize yourself doing the act. Visualize the quality accomplished. View it done.

The Limits of Bodily Visualization

When people attempt "visualization," they often imagine themselves:

- struggling,
- negotiating,
- pleading,
- worrying,
- striving,
- acting physically

❖ or forcing outcomes.

This keeps the soul anchored in bodily effort, the lowest level of intentionality. The UTC does not respond to bodily imagery. It responds to the quality of consciousness.

Imagining the physical process rather than the quality keeps the soul focused on effort, anxiety, and uncertainty.

Imagining the quality of the result creates a stable form.

Jesus' Method: Fixed Inner Completion

Jesus repeatedly teaches the inner stance of completed intention:

❖ "Whatever you ask in My name, believe you have received it."
❖ "Your faith has made you whole."
❖ "Let it be done to you according to your faith."
❖ "Peace I leave with you. My peace I give you."
❖ "The Kingdom is within you."

Each of these teachings refers to a state already formed inside consciousness:

- ❖ Peace already present.
- ❖ Forgiveness already chosen.
- ❖ Courage already embraced.
- ❖ Love already desired.
- ❖ Harmony already intended.

This is the spiritual structure behind "view it done."

Why "View It Done" Works

The UTC does not respond to emotional intensity or bodily images. It responds to quality:

- ❖ a clear desire,
- ❖ aligned with qualities,
- ❖ held without contradiction,
- ❖ offered without panic.

When the soul "views it done," it creates a stable form the UTC can receive.

Holding the quality as already chosen (already complete within you) eliminates:

- ❖ conflicted desire,
- ❖ self-doubt,
- ❖ tangled motives,
- ❖ fear of failure,
- ❖ oscillation of attention,
- ❖ mental noise.

The soul becomes coherent.

What "View It Done" Is *Not*

It is not:

- ❖ wishful thinking,
- ❖ fantasy,
- ❖ denial of reality,
- ❖ magical thinking,
- ❖ a way to evade effort,
- ❖ positive thinking,
- ❖ or self-deception.

It is not imagining circumstances. It is forming the quality you seek as already present.

What "View It Done" *Is*

It is the soul holding a finished inner state:

- ❖ "I hold peace as done."
- ❖ "I hold forgiveness as done."
- ❖ "I hold courage as done."
- ❖ "I hold reconciliation as done."
- ❖ "I hold clarity as done."
- ❖ "I hold love as done."
- ❖ "I hold humility as done."
- ❖ "I hold harmony as done."

These are qualities, not fantasies. Your prayer points to the qualities you want to be expressed as a solution to the problem you bring. Remember, the UTC and Jesus respond to and interpret qualities.

Qualities exist at the level Jesus occupies. When the soul holds a quality, it draws near to Him.

Consciousness Creates at the Level of Qualities

You are not trying to create circumstances. You are trying to invoke qualities which are compatibility with Heaven: "Jesus, please apply these qualities to this situation."

The soul becomes what it repeatedly holds in consciousness.

"View it done" means:

- ❖ stabilize the quality,
- ❖ release the fear,
- ❖ anchor the heart,
- ❖ offer the form,
- ❖ and allow the UTC to unfold events around it.

Why Saints Used This Method

The stories of the saints—East and West—repeatedly show:

255

❖ results arising quietly,
❖ healings occurring,
❖ reconciliations forming,
❖ insights appearing,
❖ peace settling over troubled hearts.

Not because they forced outcomes, but because they held qualities firmly and peacefully.

They viewed the outcome of light, not the mechanics of effort.

The Psychological Benefit

"View it done" also stabilizes the nervous system:

❖ effort increases anxiety,
❖ struggle increases resistance,
❖ fantasy increases confusion.

But inner completion creates:

❖ calm,
❖ steadiness,
❖ clear perception,
❖ grounded intention.

The Spiritual Benefit

At the spiritual level:

- ❖ desire becomes singular,
- ❖ contradictions dissolve,
- ❖ qualities amplify,
- ❖ Jesus' presence becomes clearer.

The soul is no longer split between fear and hope. It stands whole.

The Practical Method

The practice is simple: Ask Jesus to interpret a quality within a situation you have in mind.

1. Clarify the quality you desire Jesus to form in you and express through you. Name the situation briefly, then name the quality you want expressed in whatever unfolds."
2. Align it with qualities the situation needs.
3. Remove fear from the desire.
4. Hold the quality as already complete.
5. Release the intention into the UTC.
6. Act physically as led, but without anxiety.

The soul prays from completeness, not desperation.

Why This Is Not Self-Deification

You are not claiming divine powers. You are cooperating with Jesus:

- ❖ He clarifies the desire.

- ❖ He purifies the intention.
- ❖ He confirms the quality.
- ❖ He stands with you in forming the inner state.

You invoke the quality. The UTC provides the substance. Jesus governs the moral harmony of that quality produces.

Heaven Practices This Constantly

Heaven is a realm where:

- ❖ consciousness shapes form directly,
- ❖ qualities guide every act,
- ❖ intention becomes creation,
- ❖ harmony is natural.

"View it done" is Earth's training in Heaven's activity of turning qualities into forms.

The Soul's Transformation

When the soul learns to think in terms of qualities and to "view it done," it becomes:

- ❖ less reactive,
- ❖ less fearful,
- ❖ less dominated by circumstances.

And more:

- ❖ centered,
- ❖ capable,
- ❖ spiritually aligned,
- ❖ peaceful,
- ❖ clear,
- ❖ effective.

The soul becomes compatible with the life it will one day live in Heaven.

The Beginning of Divine Co-Creation

"View it done" is not about controlling the world. It is about becoming the kind of soul that Jesus can trust with creative responsibility.

It is preparation for eternity.

In the next chapter, we explore why spiritual action is slow—why the UTC unfolds through time and how Jesus trains the soul to accept this slowness without losing faith or clarity.

Chapter 33 – Time and Unfolding: Why Spiritual Action Is Slow

Spiritual action is slow. This is not a flaw in the structure of the universe—it is the very design of the Urge-to-Create (UTC) and the curriculum of Earth. Every soul must learn to live within this slowness, to trust it, to work with it, and to grow through it.

If the UTC responds to form, and if Jesus teaches us how to create form through desire and intention, why do results not appear instantly?

Because Earth Is Not Heaven

Heaven is the realm of immediate consonance: a place where intention becomes creation, where qualities shape reality directly, where time is not a barrier to meaning.

Earth is different.

Earth is:

- slow,
- sequential,
- developmental,
- dependent on conditions,
- bound by causality,
- and formed by resistance.

This slowness is intentional. It is the environment in which souls develop courage, humility, empathy, and wisdom.

The Nature of the UTC

The UTC provides substance, not speed.

What the UTC offers:

- possibility,
- structure,
- consistency,
- lawful unfolding.

What it does not offer:

- instant transformation,
- the collapse of processes,
- bypassing of growth,
- erasure of consequence.

The UTC unfolds through time because time is how consciousness grows.

Why Jesus Allows Slowness

Jesus could overturn the slow unfolding of the UTC. He does not.

He allows slowness because:

- ❖ growth requires process,
- ❖ courage requires struggle,
- ❖ empathy requires memory of pain,
- ❖ mercy requires experience,
- ❖ humility requires waiting,
- ❖ trust requires uncertainty,
- ❖ and love requires time.

Immediate results would bypass formation.

The Soul's Impatience

Human beings often pray:

"Why is nothing happening?" "Why doesn't God act now?" "Why is this taking so long?"

Behind these questions is the expectation that spiritual action should resemble physical action: direct, immediate, mechanical.

But spiritual action is not mechanical. It is formative.

What changes most quickly is the soul. What changes most slowly is the world around it.

Inner Change Precedes Outer Change

Every genuine spiritual transformation begins internally:

❖ fear dissolves before peace appears,
❖ resentment lifts before reconciliation occurs,
❖ courage strengthens before action is taken,
❖ clarity comes before the path reveals itself,
❖ love softens the heart before relationships heal.

The inner form must be stable before the outer form can appear.

The UTC cannot build around a soul that is still divided.

The Unseen Work of Unfolding

Most of the spiritual movement that results from prayer is invisible:

❖ shifting motives,
❖ dissolving illusions,
❖ clarifying desire,
❖ purifying intention,
❖ opening possibilities,
❖ softening resistance in others,
❖ arranging conditions over time.

This unfolding is delicate. It cannot be rushed.

Time Protects Us

Slowness is not punishment. Slowness is protection.

If every desire became reality instantly, souls would destroy themselves and each other. If every thought shaped the world immediately, chaos would reign.

Time allows:

* correction,
* repentance,
* reconsideration,
* healing,
* learning,
* maturation.

Time is mercy.

The Rhythm of Spiritual Action

Spiritual action follows a rhythm:

1. Clarify desire.
2. Align with qualities.
3. Hold the form as done.
4. Offer it into the UTC.
5. Live patiently in the unfolding.
6. Adjust as clarity increases.
7. Allow outcomes to emerge naturally as expressions of quality.

There is no shortcut that retains formation.

Jesus does not accelerate the UTC, but He is fully present during the unfolding.

He offers:

- ❖ encouragement,
- ❖ reassurance,
- ❖ insight,
- ❖ patience,
- ❖ companionship.

He teaches us how to hold calm intention without collapsing into fear, how to maintain alignment with qualities without becoming discouraged, how to trust the process without losing heart.

The Difference Between Delay and Denial

Delay is part of the process. Denial occurs only when desire remains incompatible with qualities or with the freedom of others.

If desire is clear, aligned, and good, delay means:

"More formation is happening. Keep walking."

The Soul Becomes Eternal Through Time

Time teaches what eternity requires:

- ❖ steadiness,
- ❖ depth,
- ❖ resilience,
- ❖ fidelity,
- ❖ humility,
- ❖ compassion.

A soul shaped by time can be trusted with eternity.

The Joy of the Slow Path

The slow path is not only necessary—it is beautiful.

It reveals:

- ❖ the soul's true capacity,
- ❖ the strength of intention,
- ❖ the depth of love,
- ❖ the integrity of desire,
- ❖ the presence of Jesus.

It teaches us that Heaven is worth becoming.

The Destiny of Slowness

When the soul enters Heaven, time becomes harmony rather than resistance.

But the character formed through waiting, the qualities developed through unfolding, the clarity gained through slowness – these become eternal.

In the next chapter, we turn from the mechanics of spiritual action to its moral core: why evil is defined as indifference to another's pain, and how this simple truth stands as the dividing line between Heaven and Hell.

Part V Good and Evil, Heaven and Hell, Earth as Curriculum

Chapter 34 – Evil as Indifference to Pain

In SC3, evil is not defined by mythic darkness, supernatural malice, or cosmic opposition to God. Evil is far simpler, far more recognizable, and far more human:

Evil is indifference to the pain of another conscious being.

This definition is not symbolic or poetic. It is literal. It is the moral axis that emerged when Jesus first witnessed some angels treating the inner life of others as negligible. It is the same axis that shapes every human choice on Earth. It is the dividing line between Heaven and Hell.

Why Pain Is the Moral Foundation

Pain is the experience of harm to sensibility. Only important things can hurt, so pain reveals what matters. It reveals:

* vulnerability,
* inner life,
* need,
* meaning,
* and the reality of consciousness.

A being who recognizes the pain of another recognizes their humanity—or their personhood, in the case of angels. A being who disregards that pain denies the value of consciousness itself.

271

This denial is the seed of all evil.

The First Evil Was Not Violence

The first evil was not a war among angels. It was not destruction or overt hostility.

The first evil was a shift in posture:

"My pain matters. Yours does not."

It was the birth of indifference.

From this simple, deadly stance flowed:

❖ pride,
❖ rivalry,
❖ deceit,
❖ domination,
❖ cruelty.

The entire structure of Hell begins with a shrug.

THE VALUING SPECTRUM

In SC3, moral direction can be read as valuing versus de-valuing. Love and hate are not merely emotions; they are declarations about the worth of being.

Love (valuing): "I am glad you and I are alive."

Hate (de-valuing): "I want you dead."

Self-hate: "I want to die."

BRIGHT LOVE → DULL LOVE → INDIFFERENCE → DULL HATE → INTENSE HATE

❖ Bright love: delight, gratitude, tenderness, compassion, protective courage.

❖ Dull love: goodwill, respect, fairness, patience, truthfulness, restraint.

❖ Indifference: numbness, neglect, dismissal, "not my problem."

❖ Dull hate: resentment, contempt, envy, scapegoating, wishing harm.

❖ Intense hate: vengeance, cruelty, dehumanization, desire to annihilate.

Pain can pull the soul toward de-valuing. SC3's daily practice is simple: locate yourself honestly on the spectrum—then choose the next quality one step toward love.

Companion resource: A printable "Valuing Spectrum" self-assessment and related exercises are available at SpiritualChristianity.com.

Why Indifference Is Worse Than Hatred

Hatred is reactive. It acknowledges the other person's existence and significance, even if violently.

Indifference erases them.

Hatred has the potential to be transformed into reconciliation. Indifference has no moral tension. It feels no pull toward compassion.

273

Jesus consistently treats indifference as more dangerous than hatred:

- ❖ The rich man ignores Lazarus.
- ❖ The priest and Levite ignore the wounded traveler.
- ❖ The goats in Matthew 25 ignore "the least of these."

The sin in each case is not aggression. It is refusal to care.

How Indifference Creates Hell

Hell is not a location created as punishment. It is a spiritual condition formed by habitual indifference.

A soul that repeatedly says:

- ❖ "Your pain does not matter,"
- ❖ "Your joy does not matter,"
- ❖ "Your existence does not matter,"

forms itself into a being incompatible with Heaven.

This incompatibility becomes isolation. Isolation becomes self-absorption. Self-absorption becomes the atmosphere of Hell.

Hell is what happens when consciousness collapses inward.

How Indifference Operates on Earth

Indifference shows up in countless forms:

- ❖ refusing to acknowledge someone's suffering,
- ❖ disregarding the emotional life of a partner or child,
- ❖ dehumanizing strangers,
- ❖ using others for advantage,
- ❖ bypassing responsibility,
- ❖ minimizing harm inflicted,
- ❖ spiritual apathy toward injustice,
- ❖ failing to intervene when someone is being hurt.

Indifference wounds not only the victim, but also the soul practicing it.

Why Jesus Cannot Tolerate Indifference

Jesus, as the first Consciousness, cannot ignore pain. He is constitutionally incapable of disregarding another's inner life.

This is why:

- ❖ He heals,
- ❖ He comforts,
- ❖ He defends,
- ❖ He teaches mercy,
- ❖ He confronts cruelty,

❖ He elevates the outcast.

He is not performing goodness. He is expressing the core of who He is.

Indifference contradicts His nature at the deepest level.

Jesus Defines Evil Through Care

Jesus does not define evil through ritual violation or doctrinal error. He defines it through failure of care:

❖ "I was hungry, and you did not feed Me."
❖ "I was thirsty, and you did not give Me drink."
❖ "I was sick, and you did not visit Me."

"Whatever you did not do to the least of these, you did not do to Me."

Evil is not merely doing harm. Evil is failing to care about harm.

Indifference as the Opposite of Heaven

Heaven is the community where:

❖ every soul respects the pain of others,
❖ every soul rejoices in the existence of others,
❖ joy is shared,
❖ empathy is natural,

❖ and love is constant.

Indifference cannot exist in such a community. It is the anti-Heaven.

A soul that takes pleasure in its own existence but not in the existence of others has no place in Heaven's harmony.

Healing Indifference

Indifference is healed by:

❖ experiencing one's own pain honestly,
❖ receiving compassion,
❖ learning empathy through relationship,
❖ confronting personal fear and numbness,
❖ awakening moral imagination,
❖ choosing qualities,
❖ walking with Jesus.

No soul is beyond healing if it is willing to see pain—its own and others'.

The Human Life as Antidote to Indifference

Not-Heaven (Earth) exposes every soul to fragility:

❖ loss,
❖ grief,
❖ illness,

❖ disappointment,

❖ failure.

These experiences help break indifference. They give the soul the capacity to say:

"I know what this pain feels like. I will not cause it in others."

This is the beginning of goodness.

The Threshold Between Heaven and Hell

The threshold is simple:

❖ If a soul respects the pain and joy of others, it moves toward Heaven.
❖ If a soul dismisses the pain and joy of others, it moves toward Hell.

Jesus' entire moral teaching rests on this distinction.

Evil Is Always a Moral Blindness

Evil is not strength. It is blindness. Blindness to sensibility. Blindness to the inner life of others. Blindness to one's own humanity.

Jesus heals this blindness with:

❖ truth,

- ❖ mercy,
- ❖ compassion,
- ❖ confrontation,
- ❖ invitation,
- ❖ and love.

Evil dissolves when indifference dissolves.

The First Question of Spiritual Life

The first moral question is not:

"What rules must I obey?"

It is:

"Do I care about the pain of others?"

The answer to this question determines the direction of the soul.

In the next chapter, we turn to the positive dimension of morality—how caring for another's sensibility and rejoicing in their existence becomes the foundation of goodness and the gateway to Heaven.

279

Chapter 35 – Goodness as Care for Sensibility

If evil is indifference to the pain of another, then goodness is its luminous opposite:

Goodness is care for the sensibility of another being—care for their pain, care for their joy, care for their inner life.

This is the entire moral architecture of SC3. This is the essence of Jesus' teaching. This is the heartbeat of Heaven.

Goodness is not rule-keeping. It is not religiosity. It is not moral performance. It is not compliance out of fear.

Goodness is the instinctive, chosen, freely embraced stance:

"Your pain matters to me, and your joy matters to me."

The Heart of Goodness

Goodness is not a behavior; it is a way of being.

A good soul:

- ❖ does not dismiss another's suffering,
- ❖ does not ignore their fear,
- ❖ does not exploit their vulnerability,

- ❖ does not envy their joy,
- ❖ does not resent their existence,
- ❖ does not withhold compassion.

Instead, a good soul:

- ❖ notices pain,
- ❖ responds with qualities,
- ❖ honors the inner life,
- ❖ protects the vulnerable,
- ❖ rejoices in another's being,
- ❖ works toward harmony.

This is goodness as Jesus defines it.

Jesus' Teaching on Goodness

Jesus' moral clarity is astonishingly simple:

- ❖ The Good Samaritan: goodness is stopping for the wounded.
- ❖ The sheep in Matthew 25: goodness is serving "the least of these."
- ❖ The Beatitudes: goodness belongs to the poor in spirit, the meek, the merciful.
- ❖ His healings: goodness lifts suffering without humiliation.
- ❖ His forgiveness: goodness restores dignity.
- ❖ His protection of the woman caught in adultery: goodness shields the shamed.

❖ His blessing of children: goodness delights in vulnerability.

Jesus never defines goodness as religious conformity. He always defines it as care.

Why Goodness Requires Sensitivity

To care for sensibility, one must be able to:

- ❖ perceive pain,
- ❖ sense fear,
- ❖ understand joy,
- ❖ respect vulnerability,
- ❖ value consciousness.

Evil numbs this sensitivity. Goodness sharpens it.

A soul trained in goodness becomes attentive:

- ❖ to the tremble of a wounded heart,
- ❖ to the joy in another's success,
- ❖ to the loneliness behind anger,
- ❖ to the anxiety beneath defensiveness.

Goodness sees deep.

The Joy Dimension of Goodness

Goodness does not only respond to pain. It also celebrates joy.

A good soul says:

"It is good that you exist. Your happiness enriches the world. Your presence brings light."

This capacity—to rejoice in another's existence—is the seed of Heaven.

Jealousy destroys joy. Goodness protects it.

Goodness and Qualities

Goodness requires qualities:

- ❖ Love to embrace another.
- ❖ Truth to see them clearly.
- ❖ Courage to act despite fear.
- ❖ Mercy to soften judgment.
- ❖ Humility to set aside ego.
- ❖ Harmony to restore connection.

Qualities are not optional accessories. They are the tools of goodness.

Without qualities, goodness collapses into sentimentality or self-righteousness.

With qualities, goodness becomes Heaven's nature expressed on Earth.

Earth gives every soul countless opportunities to learn goodness:

- ❖ in relationships,
- ❖ in family,
- ❖ in friendship,
- ❖ in conflict,
- ❖ in sorrow,
- ❖ in disappointment,
- ❖ in responsibility,
- ❖ in love.

Earth is the arena where goodness becomes real through practice:

- ❖ comforting,
- ❖ apologizing,
- ❖ forgiving,
- ❖ supporting,
- ❖ listening,
- ❖ protecting,
- ❖ encouraging,
- ❖ reconciling.

Every act of goodness leaves an imprint on the soul.

Goodness as the Path to Heaven

Heaven is the eternal community of goodness:

- ❖ pain protected,
- ❖ joy shared,
- ❖ dignity honored,
- ❖ harmony preserved.

Only souls who care about sensibility can safely live there. Not because God excludes them, but because the nature of Heaven demands compatibility.

Jesus teaches goodness because Heaven requires it.

How Goodness Heals the Soul

Every act of goodness heals something inside the one who offers it:

- ❖ kindness heals bitterness,
- ❖ compassion heals pride,
- ❖ generosity heals fear,
- ❖ forgiveness heals shame,
- ❖ gentleness heals anger,
- ❖ gratitude heals despair.

Goodness returns the soul to the joy of existence.

The Simplicity and Power of Goodness

Goodness is simple:

See the inner life of others. Honor it.

Goodness is powerful:

It stabilizes communities. It heals wounds. It binds people together. It makes Heaven possible.

The First Question of Goodness

Jesus reduces goodness to a question the soul can ask at any moment:

"Am I increasing or decreasing another's capacity for joy?"

Or its twin:

"Am I deepening or relieving another's pain?"

The answer reveals the soul's trajectory.

Goodness in the Eyes of Jesus

When Jesus looks at a soul and sees goodness—even in small form—He rejoices.

Goodness mirrors His heart. It moves the soul toward Him. It signals compatibility with Heaven.

287

In the next chapter, we explore the fullness of this compatibility—how souls grow into the joy of existence and become beings who not only refrain from harm but actively celebrate one another's being.

Chapter 36 – Toward the Joy of Existence: Moving From Indifference to Compatibility.

If evil is indifference to pain, and goodness is care for sensibility, then the destination of the soul—the full expression of compatibility with Heaven—is the joy of existence shared with others.

This is not emotional excitement. It is not pleasure or thrill. It is not circumstantial happiness.

It is the quiet, deep, foundational awareness Jesus first experienced when He awakened as the first Consciousness:

- ❖ "It is good that I exist."
- ❖ "It is good that you exist."
- ❖ "It is good that we exist together."

This joy is the atmosphere of Heaven. It is the final state toward which every soul is being formed.

Joy as the Fulfillment of Goodness

Goodness begins with:

- ❖ honoring pain,
- ❖ caring about sensibility,
- ❖ noticing vulnerability,
- ❖ responding with qualities.

289

But goodness reaches fulfillment only when the soul can also celebrate the existence of others.

This is why Jesus rejoices over:

- ❖ children,
- ❖ acts of faith,
- ❖ restored dignity,
- ❖ awakened hearts,
- ❖ forgiven sinners.

Goodness protects pain. Joy celebrates being.

Why Joy Is the Opposite of Pain

Pain says: "Something in me is harmed." Joy says: "Something in me is flourishing."

Pain reveals vulnerability. Joy reveals worth.

Pain awakens empathy. Joy awakens communion.

Pain drives the soul inward for healing. Joy draws the soul outward for relationship.

Both are essential. Both shape the soul for Heaven.

Joy as the Light of Heaven

Heaven is not merely the absence of pain. It is the fullness of joy.

In Heaven:

- ❖ every soul delights in its own existence,
- ❖ every soul delights in the existence of others,
- ❖ envy is gone,
- ❖ rivalry is gone,
- ❖ fear is gone,
- ❖ shame is gone,
- ❖ comparison is gone.

Heaven is the community where joy is mutual and constant.

Why Joy Is Difficult on Earth

Earth (Not-Heaven) wounds sensibility:

- ❖ trauma,
- ❖ loss,
- ❖ injustice,
- ❖ disappointment,
- ❖ fear,
- ❖ shame.

These wounds make joy difficult. They distort self-perception. They make it hard to accept our own existence, let alone rejoice in another's.

This is why spiritual healing is essential. The soul must recover the capacity for joy.

Jesus as the Restorer of Joy

Jesus restored joy everywhere He went:

- ❖ turning water into wine,
- ❖ feeding crowds,
- ❖ healing the sick,
- ❖ freeing the ashamed,
- ❖ dignifying the outcast,
- ❖ blessing children,
- ❖ comforting mourners,
- ❖ strengthening the fearful.

In every act, He was not only relieving pain; He was restoring joy.

He wants the soul to recover the joy of existence He knew from eternity.

Joy and Qualities

Joy requires qualities:

- ❖ Love opens the heart to others.
- ❖ Truth anchors the soul in reality.
- ❖ Courage allows vulnerability.
- ❖ Mercy heals shame.
- ❖ Humility silences comparison.
- ❖ Harmony creates community.

Without qualities, joy is unstable. With qualities, joy becomes eternal.

Joy as Freedom

Joy frees the soul:

- from fear,
- from resentment,
- from envy,
- from shame,
- from despair.

Joy stabilizes moral life. A joyful soul does not need to harm others. A joyful soul is not threatened by the joy of others.

Joy and the Soul's Identity

The soul's identity is revealed most clearly when it can say:

"I am glad I exist."

This is the healed "I." This is the echo of Jesus' first consciousness.

When the soul can also say:

"I am glad you exist,"

293

it becomes compatible with Heaven.

Joy and Eternal Community

Heaven is built on joy because joy is:

- ❖ inclusive,
- ❖ relational,
- ❖ expansive,
- ❖ creative,
- ❖ stabilizing,
- ❖ and eternal.

Jesus does not want Heaven to be populated by souls who merely avoid harm. He wants Heaven populated by souls who delight in one another.

Joy as the Soul's True Nature

The soul begins in fear. It grows in goodness. It matures in qualities. It ends in joy.

This joy is not something the soul must earn. It is something the soul must uncover, recover, and embrace.

The Invitation to Joy

Jesus invites every soul:

- ❖ to heal,
- ❖ to grow,

❖ to shed fear,

❖ to release shame,

❖ to choose qualities,

❖ to honor pain,

and to discover the deepest truth: Your existence is good. And so is the existence of every soul you meet.

This is the joy of existence—the eternal state for which every human being is made.

In the next chapter, we turn from joy to its cosmic consequence: Heaven itself, and why only souls formed in goodness and joy can live there forever.

Chapter 37 – Hell as the Community of Indifference

Hell is not a pit of fire, a realm beneath the earth, or a torture chamber created by God. In SC3, Hell is something far more profound, far more tragic, and far more psychologically real:

Hell is the community of souls who no longer care about the sensibility of others. It is the spiritual society formed by indifference.

Hell is not imposed. Hell is not inflicted. Hell is not a punishment.

Hell is the natural environment produced by beings who disregard the inner life of others— beings who either cannot or will not care about another's pain or joy.

The Genesis of Hell

Hell began long before Earth existed.

It began when some angels—created to share the joy of existence—chose indifference:

"My joy matters. Yours does not."

This stance became:

❖ pride,

- ❖ rivalry,
- ❖ self-exaltation,
- ❖ contempt,
- ❖ domination,
- ❖ and cruelty.

Not because they set out to be "evil," but because they stopped caring.

Indifference always matures into cruelty.

Hell as the Anti-Heaven

Heaven is built on:

- ❖ care for pain,
- ❖ reverence for sensibility,
- ❖ joy of existence shared.

Hell is built on the opposite:

- ❖ disregard for pain,
- ❖ contempt for vulnerability,
- ❖ joy taken only in oneself.

Heaven expands consciousness outward. Hell collapses consciousness inward.

Heaven is mutual joy. Hell is mutual indifference.

298

What Hell Feels Like

Hell is not fire; it is isolation.

Hell feels like:

- ❖ being unseen,
- ❖ being unheard,
- ❖ being unnecessary,
- ❖ being dismissed,
- ❖ being unsafe,
- ❖ being surrounded by others who do not care.

Hell is consciousness without communion.

When a soul enters Hell, nothing burns it from the outside. It burns from the inside:

because its own indifference reduces the entire universe to itself.

Why Jesus Cannot Force Heaven

Jesus cannot force a soul into Heaven for one simple reason:

A soul that does not care about the sensibility of others cannot live in Heaven without harming it.

Heaven is harmony. A soul without empathy is discord.

Heaven is shared joy. A soul that resents the joy of others destabilizes Heaven.

Heaven is relational wholeness. A soul closed in on itself cannot participate.

Jesus does not exclude such a soul. The soul excludes itself.

How Souls Drift Toward Hell

Souls drift toward Hell gradually:

- by ignoring pain,
- by preferring pride to humility,
- by choosing domination over love,
- by resenting others' joy,
- by refusing mercy,
- by hiding from truth,
- by shutting down vulnerability.

Every time a soul turns inward at the expense of others, it takes one step closer to isolation.

Hell's Social Structure

Hell is not solitary confinement. It is a community –

> – but a community made of inward-turned beings.

300

A society of:

- ❖ envy,
- ❖ suspicion,
- ❖ rivalry,
- ❖ manipulation,
- ❖ coercion,
- ❖ pride.

Each soul seeks its own advantage. Each soul suspects the others. Each soul refuses to be vulnerable. Each soul fears exploitation.

This is the spiritual physics of Hell.

Why Hell Is Suffering

Hell is suffering not because God torments souls, but because indifference destroys joy.

A soul in Hell:

- ❖ cannot rejoice in others,
- ❖ cannot receive joy from others,
- ❖ cannot trust,
- ❖ cannot be honest,
- ❖ cannot rest,
- ❖ cannot love.

Isolation becomes torment. Self-absorption becomes prison. Pride becomes misery.

Hell hurts because the soul has lost the capacity for joy.

Why Jesus Grieves Over Hell

Jesus does not hate those in Hell. He grieves for them.

He sees what they could have become— beings of joy, beings of care, beings capable of eternity.

But He also respects their choices.

Love cannot override the will. Joy cannot be forced. Care cannot be imposed.

A soul that refuses to care cannot be made to care.

Can Hell Be Left?

SC3 holds a hopeful but sober position:

A soul may leave Hell if it regains the capacity to care.

This requires the willingness to feel pain—its own and others'.

It requires humility, repentance, and qualities.

But most souls in Hell refuse this path because:

- ❖ caring feels dangerous,
- ❖ vulnerability feels unbearable,
- ❖ humility feels humiliating,
- ❖ and joy feels foreign.

Hell persists where the will refuses to soften.

Earth as the Prevention of Hell

Earth exists to prevent Hell.

Earth teaches:

- ❖ empathy through suffering,
- ❖ humility through failure,
- ❖ compassion through loss,
- ❖ joy through gratitude,
- ❖ courage through danger,
- ❖ mercy through forgiveness.

Souls who learn these lessons become safe for Heaven. Souls who refuse them drift toward Hell.

Earth is the crossroads between the two eternities.

The Soul's Final Direction

The soul's direction is simple:

- ❖ Toward Heaven if it cares about the pain and joy of others.

❖ Toward Hell if it grows indifferent.

Every moral choice is one step.

Hell Is the Logical Result of Indifference

Hell is not divine anger. It is cause and effect.

When consciousness rejects:

❖ empathy,
❖ humility,
❖ truth,
❖ mercy,
❖ love,
❖ harmony,

the result is isolation.

Hell is what beings become when they refuse to become like Jesus.

Hope Even for Hell

Even in Hell, Jesus remains the light.

He does not erase the soul. He does not abandon it. He waits.

He continues to offer:

❖ memory,

* compassion,
* invitation,
* and the possibility of turning toward sensibility.

But He will not force Heaven on anyone.

The Meaning of Hell

Hell reveals:

* the danger of indifference,
* the necessity of qualities,
* the reason for Earth,
* the seriousness of free will,
* the meaning of moral growth.

Hell is the tragic alternative to the joy Jesus intended for all beings.

In the next chapter, we will ascend from this shadow to contemplate Heaven itself— the realm of mutual joy, shared sensibility, and the eternal harmony Jesus created for those who choose love.

Chapter 38 – Why freedom is necessary and why compatibility, not reward, determines destiny.

Life is the long training in compatibility.

Eternity is the fulfillment of what the soul has chosen to become.

Those two sentences explain the entire moral architecture of the afterlife.

Heaven welcomes those who want what Heaven is. Hell holds those who refuse what Heaven contains.

The choice is not imposed from outside; it is revealed from within.

Freedom is the dignity of the soul. Compatibility is the logic of eternity.

A soul cannot be forced into Heaven because Heaven is made of qualities. A being whose inner life is dominated by deceit, cruelty, indifference, or self-absorption would not experience Heaven as joy; it would experience Heaven as torment. Not because Heaven harms, but because Heaven reveals.

Heaven is not simply where God lives. Heaven is where God's family lives together. Earth is where the soul learns how to belong to this family. Every act of love, every step toward forgiveness, every movement away

307

from isolation and toward relationship is a rehearsal for the eternal household of Heaven.

---

1. Compatibility: Why Heaven Cannot Be Imposed

Compatibility means that the nature of the soul and the nature of Heaven must resonate.

Heaven is the community where:

- ❖ pain is honored,
- ❖ joy is shared,
- ❖ qualities rule every interaction,
- ❖ and every soul delights in the existence of every other.

A soul that resents others' joy, ignores their pain, or insists on domination would not fit such a place. Heaven would feel wrong to it—too bright, too honest, too mutual, too free of control.

If such a soul were placed in Heaven by decree, it would either:

- ❖ try to bend Heaven back toward its own indifference, or
- ❖ retreat into isolation and misery.

This is why Heaven cannot be granted like a prize. Heaven must be grown into. It is not a reward given after life; it is a nature formed during life.

---

2. Freedom: The Risk and Dignity of the "I"

Freedom is the condition under which compatibility becomes real.

Without freedom, qualities cannot exist:

- Love cannot be forced.
- Compassion cannot be demanded.
- Humility cannot be imposed.
- Courage cannot be manufactured by decree.

If Jesus overrode freedom, He would also override the very process by which souls grow into maturity. A forced soul cannot love. A controlled soul cannot develop mercy or truth or generosity.

Freedom is not the obstacle to salvation; it is the condition for it.

This is why Jesus never framed eternal life as a transaction:

"Do this and you will be paid with Heaven."

Instead, He said in many ways:

"Become like Me."

Likeness is compatibility. Heaven is not granted from the outside; it emerges from within as the soul chooses qualities under real conditions of risk and vulnerability.

---

3. Heaven and Hell as Outcomes, Not Sentences

Heaven is compatibility. Hell is incompatibility.

Both are outcomes of freedom.

When a soul habitually chooses care, truth, mercy, and humility, it becomes a being who naturally moves toward Heaven's light. When a soul habitually chooses indifference, deception, contempt, or domination, it becomes a being who naturally recoils from that light.

At resurrection, nothing arbitrary happens. The soul simply encounters full revelation:

- It sees Jesus clearly.
- It sees itself clearly.
- It sees what it has become.

A soul in love with qualities runs toward the light. A soul committed to indifference retreats from it.

Jesus does not cast souls out. Souls cast themselves out by their inner resistance to qualities.

---

4. Earth as the Workshop of Compatibility

Earth is where compatibility is forged.

Every moment—ordinary or dramatic—gives the soul a choice:

* Move toward care or toward indifference.
* Move toward truth or toward self-deception.
* Move toward humility or toward pride.
* Move toward reconciliation or toward withdrawal.

The simplest everyday acts shape eternal capacity:

* A patient reply when irritated.
* A quiet apology instead of a defense.
* A hidden act of generosity.
* A difficult forgiveness chosen again and again.

No action is small when seen as material for compatibility. The soul is learning, every day, whether Heaven will one day feel like home.

5. Direction, Not Perfection

Compatibility is not about flawless performance. It is about direction.

On Earth, no soul lives qualities perfectly. We hesitate, fall back, lash out, regret, and begin again. Jesus knows this. He is not measuring perfection; He is watching direction.

The key questions are:

- When you fall, do you want to get up?
- When you harm, do you care that you harmed?
- When you see pain, does something in you want to respond?
- When you glimpse goodness, does something in you want more of it?

Even a soul with many failures can be profoundly compatible with Heaven if it loves what Heaven is made of.

Conversely, a soul with respectable behavior but a cold heart can be deeply incompatible with Heaven. Outward success without inward care does not prepare a soul for joy.

---

6. Grace as Formation, Not Exception

In SC3, grace is not a loophole in the moral structure of the universe. Grace is Jesus' ongoing work of formation inside the curriculum of Earth.

Grace means:

- ❖ Jesus never stops offering clarity about who we are.
- ❖ He never stops inviting us toward qualities.
- ❖ He never stops healing what we bring into His light.
- ❖ He never counts our failures against us when we are willing to keep learning.

Grace does not cancel compatibility; it creates it. Grace is Jesus patiently reshaping the soul until it can live in Heaven without harming it or fearing it.

7. Freedom, Desire, and Final Belonging

Freedom means that, in the end, every soul will live where it truly wants to live—

- ❖ in a universe of mutual joy, shared sensibility, and qualities (Heaven), or
- ❖ in a universe narrowed to self, indifference, and isolation (Hell).

Jesus respects this terrifying dignity. He will stand with the soul as long as there is any desire left for qualities, any tenderness left toward others, any longing left for truth.

Heaven's doors do not close because Jesus grows impatient. Heaven's doors close only where desire for Heaven has been abandoned.

---

8. The Present Choice

Right now, in the small decisions of one ordinary day, the soul is quietly answering two questions:

1. Do I want what Heaven is made of?
2. Am I willing to become that kind of being?

If the answer, even weakly, is "yes," then the entire structure of existence—Earth's curriculum, the UTC's unfolding, Jesus' gentleness and guidance—is aligned to help the soul grow into compatibility.

Life is the long training in compatibility. Eternity is the fulfillment of what the soul has chosen to become.

Heaven is simply the place where that becoming is finally complete.

Chapter 39 – Heaven as the Community of Joy

If Hell is the community of indifference, then Heaven is the community of joy. Not excitement, not pleasure, not thrill—those are emotional states. Heaven's joy is deeper: the shared, mutual recognition of the goodness of existence.

Heaven is the society in which every soul can say: "It is good that I exist, and it is good that you exist."

Heaven is the fulfilled form of Jesus' first consciousness and the completed work of His mission. It is the eternal home for souls shaped by qualities, healed of indifference, and awakened to the joy that flows from God's own being.

Heaven Begins in Jesus' First Joy

Heaven starts where Jesus started: in the moment He awakened as the first Consciousness and discovered the joy of existence.

This joy was:

- ❖ peaceful,
- ❖ stable,
- ❖ identity-affirming,
- ❖ other-affirming,

❖ relational,

❖ and eternal.

Heaven is the expansion of that joy into community.

Heaven Is Built on Two Commitments

Heaven's structure is simple and absolute:

    a. Respect for pain
    b. Rejoicing in existence

Every soul in Heaven:

❖ honors vulnerability,

❖ protects sensibility,

❖ delights in each person's being,

❖ and shares joy freely.

Without these commitments, Heaven cannot remain Heaven.

Why Only Certain Souls Can Live in Heaven

A soul that refuses to respect pain harms others. A soul that refuses to rejoice in others harms joy.

Heaven is not exclusive by decree. It is exclusive by *compatibility*.

Only souls who have learned:

- ❖ empathy,
- ❖ humility,
- ❖ mercy,
- ❖ truth,
- ❖ courage,
- ❖ harmony,
- ❖ and genuine delight in others

can live in a joy-based community forever.

Heaven Is the End of Comparison

Comparison cannot enter Heaven. It dies in the process of formation on Earth.

In Heaven:

- ❖ no one competes for worth,
- ❖ no one envies,
- ❖ no one boasts,
- ❖ no one hides,
- ❖ no one pretends.

Every soul knows its value without diminishing others.

Heaven Is the End of Fear

Fear dissolves in Heaven because:

- ❖ pain is no longer a threat,

317

- ❖ shame has been healed,
- ❖ trust is perfect,
- ❖ love is complete,
- ❖ relationships are safe.

Fear is only necessary in Not-Heaven. It has no function in Heaven.

Heaven Is the End of Secrecy

There is no secrecy in Heaven—not because privacy is abolished, but because fear is gone.

Souls who have no intention to harm have nothing to hide. Souls who have nothing to hide live in freedom.

Heaven Is the Fulfillment of Qualities

Heaven is where qualities become the natural mode of life:

- ❖ Love becomes communion.
- ❖ Truth becomes clarity.
- ❖ Courage becomes freedom.
- ❖ Mercy becomes safety.
- ❖ Humility becomes ease.
- ❖ Harmony becomes unity.

Each quality finds its fullest expression in Heaven.

Heaven Is Not Uniformity

Heaven is not sameness. It is harmony among difference.

Each soul:

* ❖ carries a unique history from Earth,
* ❖ expresses qualities differently,
* ❖ contributes to the community in a distinctive way.

Heaven values individuality because individuality reflects the creativity of Jesus.

Heaven Is Active Joy

Heaven is not passive rest. It is active participation in love and creation.

Heaven includes:

* ❖ relationships,
* ❖ creativity,
* ❖ exploration,
* ❖ learning,
* ❖ contribution,
* ❖ shared purpose,
* ❖ and expansion of joy.

Heaven is dynamic, not static.

Heaven and Jesus

Jesus is the center of Heaven not by authority but by nature.

He is:

- ❖ the first Consciousness,
- ❖ the fountain of joy,
- ❖ the source of qualities,
- ❖ the safety of every soul,
- ❖ the mirror of identity,
- ❖ the teacher of eternity.

Souls gather around Jesus because He is the one who reveals what existence truly is.

Heaven and You

Heaven is not distant. It begins in the soul every time it says:

- ❖ "Your pain matters to me."
- ❖ "Your joy matters to me."
- ❖ "Your existence is good."
- ❖ "I choose qualities."
- ❖ "I rejoice that you are."
- ❖ "I want to be like Jesus."

These moments are the seeds of Heaven.

Heaven is the home Jesus created:

- ❖ for angels who chose joy,
- ❖ for humans who learned empathy,
- ❖ for every soul that embraced qualities,
- ❖ for every consciousness that cared,
- ❖ for all beings capable of eternal harmony.

Heaven is not a reward. It is a community. A home for the fully awakened "I."

In the next chapter, we turn to the curriculum that prepares souls for this community—how Earth, with all its difficulty and beauty, shapes the eternal personality for Heaven.

Chapter 40 – The Curriculum of Earth

Heaven is the final home of souls who have learned to honor pain, rejoice in existence, and live from qualities. But Heaven cannot teach these lessons. Joy cannot teach empathy. Perfection cannot teach courage. Safety cannot teach humility. A painless world cannot teach compassion.

This is why Earth exists.

Earth is not a mistake, not a punishment, and not a cosmic accident. Earth is the curriculum by which the eternal personality is shaped.

Earth as the Training Ground for Eternal Beings

Jesus created Earth as a place where souls would:

- ❖ confront real vulnerability,
- ❖ experience real joy,
- ❖ make real choices,
- ❖ suffer real consequences,
- ❖ discover real humility,
- ❖ learn real compassion,
- ❖ and develop real courage.

Angels fell because they were created powerful without formation. Human beings rise because they are created vulnerable with formation.

Earth is the school that produces safe beings for Heaven.

Why Earth Must Include Difficulty

Difficulty is not divine anger; it is divine wisdom.

Earth includes:

- ❖ danger to teach courage,
- ❖ limitation to teach humility,
- ❖ loss to teach empathy,
- ❖ uncertainty to teach trust,
- ❖ failure to teach honesty,
- ❖ conflict to teach harmony,
- ❖ relationships to teach love,
- ❖ time to teach patience.

Without these conditions, souls would remain unformed.

Why Earth Cannot Be Heaven

If Earth were Heaven:

- ❖ free will would collapse,
- ❖ empathy would never deepen,
- ❖ courage would never awaken,
- ❖ humility would never form,
- ❖ love would never be tested,
- ❖ mercy would never be necessary,

* and souls would enter eternity fragile and unready.

Heaven is the outcome of formation. Earth is the arena of formation.

They cannot be the same.

Earth as the Practice Ground for Qualities

On Earth, every day gives opportunities to practice:

* Love – in families, friendships, conflict, sacrifice.
* Truth – in communication, self-honesty, integrity.
* Courage – in adversity, fear, loss, uncertainty.
* Mercy – in forgiveness, patience, compassion.
* Humility – in failure, limitation, listening, learning.
* Harmony – in reconciliation, cooperation, peace-making.

Qualities cannot be learned in theory. They must be lived in tension.

The Role of Pain in Formation

Pain is not the enemy of spiritual growth; it is the teacher of spiritual truth.

Pain teaches:

* vulnerability,

- ❖ empathy,
- ❖ reverence for others' inner lives,
- ❖ the importance of protection,
- ❖ the need for mercy,
- ❖ the value of love,
- ❖ the fragility of existence.

A soul that has truly known pain becomes incapable of disregarding another's.

This is what makes the soul safe for Heaven.

The Role of Joy in Formation

Joy, too, is part of Earth's curriculum.

Joy teaches:

- ❖ gratitude,
- ❖ belonging,
- ❖ beauty,
- ❖ connection,
- ❖ meaning,
- ❖ delight in existence.

Joy reminds the soul of its origin—Jesus' first joy of being.

Pain softens the heart; joy opens the heart.

Both are necessary.

Earth as a Mirror for the Soul

Earth reveals the truth of what a soul has become.

In moments of conflict, do we move toward love or domination? In moments of fear, do we choose courage or avoidance? In moments of hurt, do we offer mercy or retaliation? In moments of beauty, do we rejoice or envy? In moments of failure, do we choose humility or pride?

Earth is the mirror that shows the soul its readiness for Heaven.

Why Jesus Does Not Remove Earth's Difficulties

Jesus does not eliminate Earth's difficulties because:

- ❖ they are the structure of formation,
- ❖ they are the soil of qualities,
- ❖ they prepare the soul for eternity.

He walks with us through difficulty, but He does not abolish the curriculum.

He comforts, strengthens, guides, and heals— but He does not replace the lessons with shortcuts.

Earth as Preparation, Not Judgment

Earth is not the test before Heaven. It is the preparation before Heaven.

A soul is not judged for failing on Earth. A soul is shaped through its experiences here.

The only true failure is refusing to learn.

The Final Purpose of Earth

The purpose of Earth is simple:

To form souls who can safely and joyfully live in the eternal community of Heaven.

Earth teaches the soul:

- ❖ reverence for what pain reveals as important,
- ❖ delight in existence,
- ❖ commitment to qualities,
- ❖ the stability of the "I",
- ❖ the meaning of relationship,
- ❖ and the joy of mutual care.

In the next chapter, we explore the role of qualities in eternal life—why Heaven cannot exist without them and why they are the eternal identity of every soul who enters its joy.

Chapter 41 – The Role of Qualities in Eternal Life

If Heaven is the community of joy, then qualities are the structure that makes that joy possible. Heaven is not sustained by rules, law, fear, or obedience. It is sustained by the inner life of its inhabitants—souls who have become beings of love, truth, courage, mercy, humility, and harmony.

Qualities are not virtues added onto the soul. They are the *identity* of a soul made ready for eternity.

Why Heaven Requires Qualities

Heaven is a community, not a solitary paradise. Every soul lives in intimate relationship with others. If a soul lacks qualities, it destabilizes the entire harmony.

A being without qualities:

- would harm others unintentionally,
- would fail to recognize pain,
- would not rejoice in others' joy,
- would create fear,
- would fracture community,
- would collapse Heaven's harmony.

Qualities are required for Heaven the way oxygen is required for life.

Qualities Reflect Jesus' Own Nature

Jesus does not teach qualities as moral rules. He *embodies* them.

He is:

❖ Love in action,
❖ Truth without cruelty,
❖ Courage without aggression,
❖ Mercy without naïveté,
❖ Humility without shame,
❖ Harmony without suppression.

Qualities reflect His consciousness—the first Consciousness in the universe. To acquire qualities is to become compatible with Him.

Why Qualities Become Eternal Identity

A soul cannot carry fear, rivalry, envy, or indifference into Heaven. These would wound others.

Heaven requires souls who can say:

"I am safe for eternity. My presence will not harm another. My joy increases yours. Your joy increases mine."

This can only be true of a soul formed in qualities.

Each Quality Has an Eternal Function

- ❖ Love – the capacity to delight in another's existence.
- ❖ Truth – the capacity to see reality without distortion.
- ❖ Courage – the capacity to act in harmony even when challenged.
- ❖ Mercy – the capacity to respond to weakness without judgment.
- ❖ Humility – the capacity to remain grounded without comparison.
- ❖ Harmony – the capacity to unify rather than divide.

Each quality is necessary for the eternal community. Without any one of them, Heaven could not remain Heaven.

Qualities and the End of Rules

Rules exist only where qualities are missing. Heaven has no rules because:

- ❖ no soul needs restraint,
- ❖ no soul would harm another,
- ❖ no soul is confused,
- ❖ no soul seeks domination,
- ❖ no soul pretends or hides.

Rules are scaffolding. Qualities are the building.

Qualities and the Joy of Existence

A soul formed in qualities is capable of profound joy:

- ❖ Joy in its own existence,
- ❖ Joy in the existence of others,
- ❖ Joy in the presence of Jesus,
- ❖ Joy in the eternal community,
- ❖ Joy in creation itself.

Qualities enable joy to be *shared*, not hoarded.

How Earth Forms Qualities

Earth creates qualities through:

- ❖ adversity → courage,
- ❖ failure → humility,
- ❖ sorrow → compassion,
- ❖ conflict → harmony,
- ❖ responsibility → truth,
- ❖ forgiveness → mercy,
- ❖ relationship → love.

Qualities mature slowly, through repeated choices. Earth's difficulties are the fertile soil in which qualities grow.

Qualities as the Soul's Eternal Contribution

Each soul expresses qualities uniquely:

- ❖ one soul radiates gentleness,
- ❖ another radiates wisdom,
- ❖ another radiates courage,
- ❖ another radiates compassion.

Heaven celebrates this diversity. Each soul's qualities enrich the whole.

Why Qualities Cannot Be Faked

A soul cannot pretend its way into Heaven. Qualities are not performance; they are transformation.

A soul must:

- ❖ feel pain honestly,
- ❖ heal from shame,
- ❖ choose love over fear,
- ❖ walk in truth,
- ❖ surrender pride,
- ❖ forgive sincerely.

Only genuine qualities endure. Pretended goodness dissolves at the boundary of Heaven.

Qualities Make the Soul Indestructible

When qualities mature, the soul becomes:

❖ stable,
❖ peaceful,
❖ courageous,
❖ compassionate,
❖ humble,
❖ joyful.

Such a soul is indestructible because nothing in Heaven or Earth can corrupt it. It has become what God intended: an eternal consciousness shaped by love and truth.

The Meaning of Eternal Life

Eternal life is not endless time. It is endless quality.

It is the life Jesus first lived:

❖ a life of joy,
❖ a life of care,
❖ a life of harmony.

Jesus invites every soul to become like Him—not in power, but in qualities.

The Call of Jesus

Jesus' call is simple:

"Become like Me in what you love, in what you value, in how you see others, in how you treat their pain, in how you rejoice in their existence."

Qualities are the doorway to Heaven because qualities are Heaven's nature.

In the next chapter, we explore how the soul becomes compatible with Heaven—how qualities reshape identity until the soul can live forever in joy without ever harming another being.

Part VI Heaven: Resurrection, Family, and Eternal Growth

337

Chapter 42 – Resurrection and Full Revelation

Resurrection is usually imagined as something happening to the body – a corpse stirred, a grave opened, a human form made immortal. In SC3, resurrection reaches deeper. It is not first about matter; it is about consciousness.

Resurrection is the moment when the soul comes fully awake.

It is the passage from partial awareness to clear sight, from dim guessing to unveiled truth, from living behind the veil of Earth to living before the face of Jesus without distortion.

Resurrection is not the beginning of eternal life. It is the recognition of eternal life. The soul has always been eternal; resurrection is when it finally knows itself as such.

1. Life Under the Veil

While we live in Not-Heaven, consciousness functions under a necessary veil.

We see, but not fully. We know ourselves, but only in fragments. We remember, but selectively and defensively. We interpret, but our interpretations are colored by fear, shame, ego, and confusion.

This veil is not a punishment; it is protection. A fragile "I" cannot bear full exposure too soon. The curriculum of Earth needs room for:

- ❖ gradual learning,
- ❖ partial understanding,
- ❖ trial and error,
- ❖ imperfect motives,
- ❖ slow growth.

The veil allows the soul to be in formation without having to face, all at once, the entire weight of who it has become.

2. What Death Changes

Death removes nothing essential from the soul. It simply:

- ❖ releases the body,
- ❖ ends the curriculum of Earth,
- ❖ and lifts the veil.

Consciousness continues. Memory continues. Identity continues. Desire continues. Qualities—or their absence—continue.

The moment after death is not blankness. It is intensification.

Everything that was faint becomes vivid. Everything that was half-seen becomes obvious. Everything that was postponed comes into focus.

3. The First Moments of Resurrection

In the first moments after death, every soul experiences a cluster of revelations:

1. A return of full clarity of consciousness. The fog of fatigue, illness, distraction, and bodily limitation is gone. The "I" feels awake in a way it never did on Earth.

2. Recognition of one's true identity. The soul suddenly sees, "This is what I am." Not the story, not the mask, not the wounds—the consciousness itself.

3. A truthful memory of life. Not a replay designed to condemn, but a whole, coherent seeing of one's earthly journey: the choices, the turning points, the repeated patterns.

4. The unfiltered presence of Jesus. The soul realizes that the Presence dimly felt on Earth—the still, gentle companionship in conscience and suffering—was Him all along. Now He is no longer subtle.

5. The awareness of direction. Without anyone issuing a sentence, the soul feels the trajectory it has chosen: toward qualities and care, or toward indifference and isolation.

Nothing external needs to be announced. The soul recognizes itself.

4. Jesus as Light, Not Prosecutor

In resurrection, Jesus does not appear as a cosmic judge seated behind a bench, pronouncing penalties. He appears as light.

His very being reveals:

- ❖ what is true,
- ❖ what is loving,
- ❖ what is merciful,
- ❖ what is courageous,
- ❖ what is humble,
- ❖ what is harmonious.

Standing in that light, every soul simply knows:

"Here is what I became on Earth."

There is no courtroom exchange, no argument to win, no technicality to escape through. There is only truth.

For a soul formed in qualities, this light is joy. For a soul formed in indifference, this same light is unbearable.

The difference is not in Jesus. The difference is in the soul.

5. Full Revelation of One's Life

Resurrection includes a comprehensive but merciful review of life.

The soul sees:

- ❖ every moment when it honored another's sensibility,
- ❖ every act of care, protection, and courage,
- ❖ every instance of mercy, even when clumsy,
- ❖ every choice to tell the truth when lying would have been easier,
- ❖ every sacrifice made for love.

These are seen not as merits to be tallied, but as evidence: "This is who you were becoming."

The soul also sees:

- ❖ every dismissal of pain,
- ❖ every calculated cruelty or casual neglect,
- ❖ every moment of willful indifference,

* every time another's joy was resented,
* every chance to repair that was refused.

Again, not as ammunition for accusation, but as clear data about the direction of the soul.

Resurrection is radiology for the spirit. The inner structure is made visible.

6. Shame, Pride, and the Gaze of Jesus

In that light, shame and pride respond very differently.

* Shame says, "I am my worst moments. I cannot bear to be seen."
* Pride says, "I did nothing wrong. I will not bow to this truth."

Jesus' gaze breaks shame but exposes pride.

When a soul sees its failures in His presence and also feels His unshaken regard, something beautiful can happen:

"I was often foolish, frightened, selfish—and still You wanted me."

Shame begins to melt. The soul can finally accept mercy it only partially trusted on Earth.

But where the will is rigidly committed to self-importance and indifference, the same gaze feels intolerable. Pride cannot survive in truth, so it flees truth.

Heaven is where shame has been healed and pride has been relinquished. Hell is where pride clings to itself in the face of full revelation.

7. Sorting, Not Sentencing

In traditional language, resurrection is followed by "judgment." In SC3, judgment is best understood as unavoidable self-revelation in the presence of Jesus.

- A soul that loves qualities and cares about sensibility moves spontaneously toward Him.
- A soul that clings to indifference and self-absorption moves away from Him.

He does not push anyone into Heaven or Hell. Souls sort themselves by compatibility.

His light does not change them; it shows them.

This is why Heaven and Hell are not arbitrary rewards and punishments but the natural outworking of what the soul is.

8. What Becomes of the Body

Resurrection is often imagined as a perfected version of the earthly body. SC3 reads the language of "resurrection body" as a way of pointing toward fully realized consciousness rather than biological tissue.

The resurrected "body" is:

- ❖ the soul's stable, coherent identity,
- ❖ entirely free from distortion and fragmentation,
- ❖ fully capable of expressing qualities without inner resistance,
- ❖ no longer constrained by the vulnerabilities of flesh.

Jesus' own resurrection appearances hint at this:

- ❖ He is the same person, recognizable in His manner and love.
- ❖ He is continuous with His earthly life – wounds remembered, story intact.
- ❖ He is also free from ordinary limitations: appearing, disappearing, passing through locked doors.

What has been risen is not mere tissue; what has been risen is the person, fully awake.

9. The Two Experiences of the Same Light

Imagine two souls entering this unveiled state.

One has struggled, failed often, hurt others at times – but kept returning to qualities, kept asking for mercy, kept learning to care. It has been shaped by pain into empathy, by limitation into humility, by joy into gratitude.

For this soul, resurrection feels like this:

- ❖ "Everything finally makes sense.
- ❖ I was clumsy, but You were with me.
- ❖ All along, You were forming me for this."

There is relief, recognition, and an explosion of gratitude.

Another soul has cultivated indifference—using others, dismissing pain, pursuing self-advantage, laughing at mercy, evading truth.

For this soul, the same light feels like this:

- ❖ "I cannot stand this clarity.
- ❖ I do not want this kind of world.
- ❖ I do not want to belong to a community built on care."

Nothing external punishes this soul. Its own orientation makes the light unendurable.

Resurrection is one event with two possible experiences, depending on the soul's compatibility with Heaven.

10. Full Revelation and Freedom

Full revelation does not erase freedom; it completes freedom.

On Earth, choices are made under partial knowledge:

* ❖ "I did not fully see what I was doing."
* ❖ "I did not grasp the weight of that indifference."
* ❖ "I did not understand how much this mattered."

After resurrection, the soul understands. Its earlier choices are revealed for what they were – but now, in the light, a new choice emerges:

"Given what I now see, what do I want to be?"

A soul that yields to this light may allow Jesus to heal what still can be healed, to cleanse what can be cleansed, to draw it fully into Heaven.

A soul that rejects this light chooses isolation, which is the essence of Hell.

Freedom is not removed at death; it is intensified.

---

11. Resurrection as the Goal of the Curriculum

Everything in the curriculum of Earth points toward this moment.

- ❖ The development of the "I,"
- ❖ the slow awakening to qualities,
- ❖ the repeated confrontations with pain,
- ❖ the invitations to mercy,
- ❖ the chances to tell the truth,
- ❖ the opportunities to rejoice in others' existence –

All of it is preparation for full revelation in Jesus' presence.

Resurrection is the hour when the training is reviewed and the soul is ready (or not) for Heaven's community of joy.

This is why Jesus' concern is always formation, not performance. He is not tallying rules kept; He is shaping a being who can one day stand in full light without needing to flee.

12. Living Now in the Light of Then

Resurrection is not only a future event; it is a present orientation.

To live spiritually now is to begin practicing for that unveiled moment:

> ❖ allowing Jesus to show us our motives,
> ❖ letting Him expose where we are indifferent,
> ❖ receiving His mercy for our failures,
> ❖ choosing qualities even when no one sees,
> ❖ treating every person as an eternal consciousness whom we will one day see again in clear light.

We are, in a sense, rehearsing for full revelation every time we:

> ❖ confess honestly,
> ❖ forgive sincerely,
> ❖ admit truth we have avoided,
> ❖ allow compassion to interrupt our indifference.

Each of these is a small resurrection of consciousness in advance of the great one.

13. Jesus' Own Resurrection as Promise

Jesus' resurrection in history is not only the vindication of His mission; it is the prototype for ours.

In Him we see:

- ❖ that consciousness survives death,
- ❖ that identity is preserved,
- ❖ that love goes through death and comes out the other side,
- ❖ that qualities are not swallowed by darkness,
- ❖ that joy is stronger than the grave.

His empty tomb is not a magic trick; it is the sign that the curriculum will not end in meaninglessness.

The One who first discovered the joy of existence has gone through death and come back to say:

"You were made for more than Not-Heaven. You were made for full revelation, for Heaven's community, for the joy that never ends."

Resurrection and full revelation, then, are not a threat to fear but a reality to prepare for. Jesus is not waiting there with a verdict. He is walking with us here as a teacher, healer, and brother—forming souls who will be able, when the veil finally falls, to step into His light and say with joy:

"I am finally myself, and I am finally home."

Chapter 43 – Heaven's Community: Mutual Joy

Heaven is not simply a destination; it is a community—a conscious, relational, eternal society built on the joy of existence shared among beings who have become fully compatible with one another. Heaven is the fulfillment of everything Jesus experienced in His first moment of consciousness: the joy of being, the joy of others' being, and the joy of being together.

Heaven is the environment where the inner life of every soul becomes a gift to every other soul.

Heaven Is Built on Mutual Joy

Mutual joy is the core of Heaven's atmosphere:

- ❖ "It is good that I exist."
- ❖ "It is good that you exist."
- ❖ "It is good that we exist together."

Mutual joy is not emotional excitement. It is the deep, peaceful delight that arises when each soul recognizes:

1. The goodness of its own existence,
2. The goodness of the existence of others,
3. The beauty of living in harmony with all.

This joy is not fragile or fleeting. It is eternal because it is grounded in qualities.

The Three Dimensions of Heavenly Joy

Heaven's joy is:

- ❖ Personal – each soul knows its own worth.
- ❖ Interpersonal – each soul rejoices in others' worth.
- ❖ Communal – the entire community celebrates the harmony of all.

These three dimensions create a joy that cannot be shaken.

Mutual Joy Requires Qualities

Mutual joy is possible only because every soul in Heaven is formed by qualities:

- ❖ Love delights in others.
- ❖ Truth sees others clearly.
- ❖ Courage protects others.
- ❖ Mercy restores others.
- ❖ Humility honors others.
- ❖ Harmony unites others.

Without qualities, joy cannot be shared. Without qualities, Heaven cannot exist.

Why Heaven Cannot Include Indifference

Indifference is the opposite of mutual joy. A soul that does not care about others:

- ❖ cannot rejoice in them,
- ❖ cannot celebrate their being,
- ❖ cannot protect their joy,
- ❖ cannot live without harming others.

Such a soul would break Heaven. This is why compatibility is essential.

Heaven Is Transparent

Heaven has no secrets—not because privacy is forbidden, but because fear has vanished and trust is complete.

Souls can be fully known and fully loved. Nothing needs to be hidden.

Transparency is possible because:

- ❖ no one envies another,
- ❖ no one wishes harm,
- ❖ no one misuses knowledge,
- ❖ no one competes for worth.

This transparency deepens joy.

Heaven Is Relational

Heaven is not solitary bliss. It is a living, dynamic network of relationships:

- ❖ shared understanding,
- ❖ shared joy,
- ❖ shared purpose,
- ❖ shared creativity,
- ❖ shared love.

Each soul enriches the others. Each soul amplifies the joy of the others.

Heaven Is Creative

The joy of Heaven overflows into creativity:

- ❖ new ideas,
- ❖ new forms,
- ❖ new expressions of love,
- ❖ new harmonies,
- ❖ new possibilities.

Heaven expands endlessly because joy expands endlessly.

This creativity is not forced. It arises naturally from mutual joy.

Heaven Is Peace

Peace in Heaven is not the absence of conflict. It is the presence of harmony:

- ❖ every heart aligned with qualities,

356

- ❖ every soul oriented toward care,
- ❖ every intention shaped by love.

This peace is living, active, and relational.

Jesus as the Center of Heaven

Jesus is the center of Heaven not by authority but by nature:

- ❖ His joy radiates outward,
- ❖ His qualities shape the community,
- ❖ His love holds the whole together.

Heaven is the expansion of His consciousness into community form.

Souls gather around Him because in Him they recognize the truth of who they are and who they are becoming.

Heaven Honors Individuality

Heaven is unity without uniformity. Each soul brings:

- ❖ a unique story,
- ❖ a unique personality,
- ❖ a unique expression of qualities,
- ❖ a unique contribution to the whole.

Difference enriches Heaven. Uniformity would diminish it.

Heaven Is Safe

Heaven is eternally safe because:

- ❖ no soul intends harm,
- ❖ no soul envies another's joy,
- ❖ no soul dominates or deceives,
- ❖ no soul hides or withdraws.

Safety is not enforced; it is the natural result of qualities.

Heaven Is Joy Without End

Joy in Heaven is unending because:

- ❖ it is shared,
- ❖ it is relational,
- ❖ it is grounded in truth,
- ❖ it is sustained by qualities,
- ❖ it is aligned with Jesus,
- ❖ it is free from fear,
- ❖ it is free from pain.

It increases forever because it is not dependent on circumstance.

Heaven Begins Before Death

Heaven begins the moment a soul:

- ❖ delights in its own existence,
- ❖ delights in the existence of others,
- ❖ honors pain,
- ❖ rejoices in joy,
- ❖ chooses qualities,
- ❖ becomes compatible with Jesus.

Heaven begins here and continues there.

The Purpose of Heaven

Heaven is the eternal community Jesus created for:

- ❖ angels who chose joy,
- ❖ humans who learned to care,
- ❖ all beings who honor sensibility,
- ❖ all souls who rejoice in existence.

Heaven is not a reward. It is the home of souls who have become capable of eternal joy.

In the next chapter, we explore the future—how Heaven's community expands, how consciousness continues to grow, and how the soul participates in eternal creation alongside Jesus.

Chapter 44 – Heaven as Family: Why Jesus Calls Us Brothers and Sisters

Jesus did not enter the world to create followers, subjects, or admirers in the ordinary sense. He came to create family. The most astonishing titles He gives to those who desire Him are not "servants" or even "disciples," but brothers and sisters. This language is not poetic or symbolic—it reveals the deepest intention of His mission: Jesus intends to share His life, His nature, His work, and His eternal future with awakened souls.

In Spiritual Christianity 3, Jesus calls humanity brothers and sisters because His purpose is not domination but kinship. He is forming a community of equals in love—equals not in power, but in relationship, dignity, and belonging. He did not come to rule over frightened beings. He came to welcome conscious souls into the family of God.

1. Brother and Sister Language Reveals Divine Intention

    When Jesus calls us brothers and sisters, He is revealing God's desire for intimacy, companionship, shared life, and true family. This is not metaphor—it is the architecture of Heaven. Heaven is a family, not a hierarchy.

2. Brothers and Sisters Share a Common Nature

    To call someone a brother or sister means:

"We share something essential."
"We come from the same source."
"We belong to the same life."

Jesus awakens in humanity the qualities of His own nature—love, truth, courage, mercy, humility, and harmony. These qualities form spiritual kinship. Compatibility creates family resemblance.

3. Brothers and Sisters Share Mutual Recognition

    Earthly siblings recognize each other by resemblance and shared history. Spiritual siblings recognize each other by qualities, light, desire, and affinity. Souls who desire Jesus recognize His voice, His presence, His goodness, and His truth. Recognition is the bond of spiritual family.

4. Brothers and Sisters Are Heirs Together

    Jesus calls His followers "co-heirs." Co-heirs share inheritance, responsibility, purpose, and joy.

    What is Jesus' inheritance?

    Divine presence, eternal life, the qualities of Heaven, the joy of God, participation in creation, and the entire community of saints. He intends to share all of it—literally.

5. Brothers and Sisters Participate in the Same Work

    A family works together. Jesus says, "My Father is working until now, and I am working." He invites us to:

    ❖ love with Him,

- ❖ bless with Him,
- ❖ heal with Him,
- ❖ reveal truth with Him,
- ❖ uplift with Him,
- ❖ and create with Him.

6. Brothers and Sisters Share Eternal Companionship

Heaven is a community of souls who love the same qualities, delight in the same truth, honor the same goodness, desire the same presence, and participate in the same eternal life.

Jesus awakens in His companions the desires needed for eternal relationship

7. Brotherhood and Sisterhood Require Freedom.

No one can be forced into spiritual family.

Love requires freedom, willingness, desire, and sincerity.

Jesus never says, "You must be My brother." He says, "Whoever does the will of My Father is My brother and sister."

Kinship is formed in the will

8. Jesus' Gentleness Was Designed for Family.

Jesus came gently because frightened souls cannot love, intimidated souls cannot trust, and pressured souls cannot join a family. The family of God grows through invitation, recognition, desire, and awakening.

Gentleness is the environment of spiritual kinship.

9. Brothers and Sisters Grow Into His Likeness.

Family resemblance emerges through shared values, shared qualities, shared desires, and shared love. The more the soul desires Jesus, the more it becomes like Him. His family is defined by likeness, not blood.

To be saved is to be welcomed home into that family, bearing a likeness formed through vulnerability, choice, qualities, and the patient guidance of Jesus.

Heaven is not simply where God lives. Heaven is where God's family lives together.

Earth is where the soul learns how to belong to this family. Every act of love, every step toward forgiveness, every movement away from isolation and toward relationship is a rehearsal for the eternal household of Heaven.

To belong to Heaven's family is to enter a circle of mutual recognition: Jesus sees us and we see Him. We see one another as fellow heirs of the same life. The bonds of this family cannot be broken by death, time, or distance. They are anchored in the eternal life of God.

Jesus Himself is the center of this family. He is the firstborn among many siblings, the One whose life defines what it means to belong. He does not stand apart in cold superiority; He stands within as the eldest Brother, the One who went first, the One who made the way.

In Heaven, no one is isolated. No one is forgotten. No one is unnecessary. Each member of the family has a place, a contribution, a recognized value. Every story of suffering overcome, every lesson of compassion learned, every act of faithfulness completed becomes part of the shared memory and joy of Heaven.

Unity in Heaven does not erase individuality. In fact, individuality is what makes family richness possible. Each soul brings its own history, its own story of becoming, its own distinct expression of qualities into the shared life of Heaven. The harmony of Heaven is not monotony; it is coordinated difference.

In a human family, resemblance is often physical— eyes, voice, posture, gestures. In Heaven's family, resemblance is spiritual. Souls who have chosen qualities come to reflect the same inner light, the same love of goodness, the same joy of existence that lives in Jesus.

As qualities deepen, resemblance increases. As resemblance increases, belonging deepens.

Family identity in Heaven is built on resemblance. Souls become like Jesus in qualities: love, mercy, humility, truth, courage, purity, compassion, and joy. This likeness is not imposed from the outside; it is grown from the inside as the soul responds to the guidance of Jesus in Not-Heaven.

Jesus calls us His brothers and sisters because He shares His own life with us. We are not merely creatures living under His rule; we are kin invited into His inner circle. The life that began in Him—consciousness awakened in the Creative Urge—becomes the life that flows through us. This is what makes Heaven a family, not merely a kingdom.

Family is more than proximity. It is shared identity, shared nature, shared affection, and shared purpose. In Heaven, this is what binds souls together. They do not simply live near one another; they belong to one another.

Heaven is not only a community; it is a family. Jesus did not come merely to gather followers, citizens, or servants. He came to gather brothers and sisters, sons and daughters, a household that shares His life forever.

10. SC3 Summary

Jesus calls humanity "brothers and sisters" because His mission is relational, His goal is kinship, His method is gentleness, His invitation is freedom, His purpose is co-creation, and His destiny is shared life.

Heaven is a family, not a throne room.

Jesus is the firstborn among many brothers and sisters.

Every soul who desires Him is being shaped for eternal kinship.

Jesus does not seek servants – He seeks family.

He seeks you.

Heaven is not only a place where good beings gather. Heaven is a family.

Jesus did not spend His life on Earth recruiting followers, building an institution, or constructing a distant kingdom populated by obedient subjects. He spent His life looking for brothers and sisters—souls who could share His life, His nature, His future, and His joy.

Heaven is where that search is fulfilled.

In the earlier chapters we saw that Heaven is:

- the community of joy,
- the home of souls who respect pain and rejoice in existence,
- the realm where qualities are the inner structure of every person.

Now we see what all of that was for: Jesus is forming a family.

1. From Kingdom to Household

Religious language often emphasizes "kingdom": God as ruler, people as subjects, Heaven as a perfectly governed realm. There is truth in this image—but it is not the deepest truth.

A kingdom can be:

- distant,
- impersonal,
- transactional,
- focused on law and order.

A family is different. A family is:

- intimate,
- relational,
- affectionate,
- rooted in shared life rather than mere compliance.

Jesus uses both images, but when He wants to reveal God's heart, He leans toward family:

- "Our Father..."
- "Your Father knows what you need..."

❖ "Whoever does the will of My Father is My brother and sister…"

In SC3, this is not sentimental language. It is structural. Heaven is not simply where God lives; Heaven is where God's family lives together.

2. What Makes a Family?

On Earth, families are often fragile and wounded. Some are sources of love; others are sources of harm. So before we can speak of Heaven as family, we must clarify what family means in its healed, eternal sense.

A true family has at least five elements:

1. Shared origin – a common life at the root of every member.
2. Shared likeness – a recognizable resemblance, not just in appearance but in character.
3. Shared belonging – no one is extra; each person is wanted.
4. Shared memory – stories held in common, interpreted in love.
5. Shared purpose – a life lived with and for one another.

Heaven contains all five, perfectly.

❧ The shared origin is Jesus' own life, the consciousness that awakened in the Urge-to-Create.

❧ The shared likeness is qualities.

❧ The shared belonging is unbreakable kinship.

❧ The shared memory is the redeemed story of Earth.

❧ The shared purpose is eternal co-creation in joy.

Earthly families dimly echo this, sometimes beautifully, sometimes painfully. Heaven is the reality those echoes were pointing toward.

3. Shared Origin: One Life in Many Souls

In SC3, every conscious being—angelic or human—exists because Jesus, the first "I," chose to share the joy of existence. He is the fountain of personhood, the pattern of what an "I" is meant to be.

To call humans His brothers and sisters means:

The same kind of life that awakened in Him has been given, in smaller form, to you.

Not in power, not in scope, but in kind. Your consciousness is related to His.

- ❖ He is the first Self.
- ❖ You are a younger self.
- ❖ He is the original joy of existence.
- ❖ You are a developing echo of that joy.

Family begins here: in shared being.

In Heaven, this shared origin is no longer dim or theoretical. Every soul feels it. Each person knows:

"The life in me began in Him. I am not an outsider invited in as a guest. I am kin."

4. Shared Likeness: Qualities as Family Resemblance

In human families, resemblance is often physical: eyes, voice, posture, gesture. In Heaven's family, resemblance is spiritual.

Souls resemble Jesus in:

- ❖ love that genuinely delights in others,
- ❖ truthfulness that does not wound,
- ❖ courage that protects rather than dominates,
- ❖ mercy that restores rather than excuses,
- ❖ humility that rests securely in identity,

371

> ❖ harmony that draws people together rather than controlling them.

This likeness is not imposed from outside; it grows from inside as the soul repeatedly chooses qualities in Not-Heaven.

On Earth, family resemblance is often mixed with dysfunction: a shared temper, a shared insecurity, a shared wound.

In Heaven, resemblance is entirely formed by goodness. Souls look like Jesus because they have learned to want what He wants, love what He loves, and care as He cares.

To be "saved" in SC3 is to have your consciousness gradually remade until the family resemblance is unmistakable.

5. Shared Belonging: No One Extra

In many earthly families, children wonder:

> ❖ "Do I really belong here?"
> ❖ "Would I be wanted if I were different?"
> ❖ "Am I only valued if I perform?"

Heaven's family is the opposite.

Because each soul has been formed through vulnerability, choice, and qualities, every person arrives at Heaven as a distinct gift to the others. No two stories are the same. No two hearts carry the same pattern of growth, wounds, healing, and love.

In Heaven:

- no one is background;
- no one is replaceable;
- no one is tolerated;
- no one is asked to become someone else to belong.

Belonging is not earned; it is recognized.

The family sees you and says:

"We know your story. We know your courage. We know your wounds and how you walked through them. We are glad you are here. We would be less ourselves without you."

Hell isolates. Heaven includes.

Hell is the community of indifference. Heaven is the family of recognition.

6. Shared Memory: Earth Remembered in Love

Families are held together by stories:

✦ "Remember when we...?"

✦ "Do you remember how hard that season was?"

✦ "Do you remember how we got through that?"

Heaven's family shares the entire memory of Earth—but illuminated.

Nothing of the soul's history is erased. What changes is the interpretation.

- Wounds are remembered, but as the birthplace of compassion.
- Failures are remembered, but as the soil of humility.
- Losses are remembered, but as the path that opened the heart to others.
- Acts of kindness are remembered, but now seen for their full weight.
- Hidden faithfulness is remembered, finally brought into the light.

In Hell, memory torments because it is held without mercy or hope. In Heaven, memory consoles because it is held in truth and mercy at once.

The family lives inside a shared story:

"We came through Not-Heaven together. We learned qualities under pressure. We stumbled, were healed, and became who we now are."

Your life becomes part of the family's joy forever.

7. Shared Purpose: Co-Heirs, Co-Workers

A human family is healthiest when it shares purpose – not just co-existing, but collaborating:

- ❖ raising children,
- ❖ caring for one another,
- ❖ building something together.

Heaven's family shares an eternal purpose: to live in, express, and expand the joy of existence that first lived in Jesus.

This includes:

- ❖ learning each other's stories,
- ❖ deepening relationships without end,
- ❖ exploring the depths of God's creativity,
- ❖ participating with Jesus in new acts of creation,
- ❖ serving and blessing new souls who awaken into Heaven,

> * stewarding the harmony of the community.

Scripture's language of "co-heirs" and "reigning with Christ" is not about hierarchy; it is about shared work. Family members join the eldest Brother in the ongoing project of love.

You are not invited to Heaven as a permanent guest watching Jesus work. You are invited as kin who share His purpose.

8. The End of Orphanhood

Many human beings live as spiritual or emotional orphans:

> * no stable place of belonging,
> * no one who really knows their inner life,
> * no sense of being wanted,
> * no enduring "home."

Some grew up in harmful families; some lost their families; some never experienced family at all.

Jesus' mission is to end orphanhood.

On Earth, He does this by:

> * moving toward the lonely,

- ❖ dignifying the disregarded,
- ❖ forming communities of care,
- ❖ awakening in the soul the sense, "You are not alone."

In Heaven, orphanhood disappears entirely.

The soul that once wondered, "Is there any place where I truly belong?" discovers:

"This is what I was made for. This is the family I was always moving toward, even when I did not have language for it."

9. Training for Family Life on Earth

Earth is not Heaven, but it is rehearsal for Heaven's family.

Where does the soul learn to live as family?

- ❖ in imperfect churches,
- ❖ in friendships that survive tension,
- ❖ in marriages that grow through forgiveness,
- ❖ in communities that carry one another's burdens,
- ❖ in small acts of loyalty,
- ❖ in choosing to see another's inner life and care.

Often these experiences are frustrating:

> ❖ people disappoint us,
> ❖ groups fracture,
> ❖ communities wound as well as heal.

Yet even these failures are part of the training. They teach:

> ❖ how much qualities matter,
> ❖ how costly indifference is,
> ❖ how necessary forgiveness is,
> ❖ how deep the longing for real family runs.

Every time a soul chooses:

> ❖ to apologize instead of harden,
> ❖ to listen instead of dismiss,
> ❖ to stay engaged instead of withdraw,
> ❖ to rejoice in another's joy instead of envy it,

it practices Heaven's family style in Not-Heaven's conditions.

Earth is where the soul learns how to belong to a family that has never yet fully existed on Earth—but will exist forever in Heaven.

10. Individuality Inside Family

Heaven's family does not erase individuality. It completes it.

On Earth, individuality is often defended against family:

> ❖ "I must separate to be myself."
> ❖ "I must protect my uniqueness by keeping distance."

That is often necessary here, because family can be intrusive or controlling.

In Heaven, the opposite is true:

> ❖ The more you are known, the more your uniqueness is honored.
> ❖ The more you belong, the more your individuality thrives.
> ❖ The more you resemble the family in qualities, the more your particular story shines.

Everyone shares the same qualities, but no one expresses them in the same way.

> ❖ One soul expresses love mainly as tenderness; another as courage.

❖ One expresses truth as quiet wisdom; another as bright clarity.

❖ One expresses mercy as patient listening; another as bold advocacy.

The family does not flatten differences; it orchestrates them.

11. Jesus at the Center of the Family

In a human home, there is usually someone who quietly holds things together:

❖ the one who remembers,
❖ the one who reconciles,
❖ the one who welcomes,
❖ the one who keeps the table open.

In Heaven, that One is Jesus. He is:

❖ the firstborn among many siblings,
❖ the original joy of existence,
❖ the source of qualities,
❖ the mender of every "I",
❖ the storyteller of every life,
❖ the host of the eternal household.

He is not the distant head of a religious institution. He is the eldest Brother who has always wanted family, the

One who left Heaven's safety to find His siblings in Not-Heaven and bring them home.

His presence is what makes Heaven feel like home rather than simply a perfect environment.

12. What It Means to Be Saved

In SC3, to be "saved" is not primarily:

> ❖ to pass a moral test,
> ❖ to escape punishment,
> ❖ to obtain a legal status.

To be saved is:

> ❖ to become compatible with Heaven's family,
> ❖ to let Jesus form qualities in you,
> ❖ to awaken to your true "I",
> ❖ to learn to honor pain and rejoice in existence,
> ❖ to be welcomed into a circle of mutual recognition and joy.

Salvation is family readiness.

Eternal life is family life.

Heaven is the household of Jesus, filled with beings who have become His brothers and sisters in qualities, and who now share His joy forever.

Chapter 45 – The Meaning of SC3

SC3 is not a new religion, a new doctrine, or a new cosmology for its own sake. It is a way of understanding the story of existence—its origin, its struggle, its purpose, its present, and its destiny—through a single unifying lens:

Consciousness shaped for Heaven.

SC3 explains how Jesus, the first Consciousness, creates a pathway for all other conscious beings—angels and humans—to enter the community of mutual joy that Heaven is. It clarifies why Earth exists, why pain matters, why qualities matter, and why free will is essential. It interprets Scripture, experience, and existence in one coherent vision.

The Core Insight of SC3

At its heart, SC3 teaches:

You are consciousness, and your eternal destiny depends on what your consciousness becomes.

Everything else—religion, morality, suffering, prayer, technology—is secondary to this central truth.

SC3 explains three things traditional religion leaves unresolved:

1. Why did angelic rebellion occur? Because consciousness not yet formed can choose indifference.

2. Why was Earth created? To provide a curriculum for forming consciousness into safe, eternal beings.

3. What determines Heaven or Hell? Compatibility—not reward or punishment.

SC3 proposes a universe in which God does not punish or abandon; beings sort themselves according to their inner nature.

The Nature of Jesus in SC3

Jesus is not only a historical figure or a divine teacher. He is:

- the first self-aware being,
- the discoverer of the joy of existence,
- the origin of qualities,
- the architect of Heaven,
- the mender of consciousness,
- the mirror of identity,
- the guide of desire,
- the shepherd of the "I."

384

SC3 understands Jesus not merely as Savior, but as the template of consciousness itself.

The Meaning of Heaven

Heaven is not a reward. It is a community of beings who have become:

- ❖ safe,
- ❖ gentle,
- ❖ truthful,
- ❖ humble,
- ❖ merciful,
- ❖ courageous,
- ❖ harmonious,
- ❖ joyful.

Heaven is the expansion of Jesus' first joy: "It is good that I exist, and it is good that you exist."

The Meaning of Hell

Hell is not punishment. It is the natural consequence of a soul that chooses:

- ❖ indifference,
- ❖ pride,
- ❖ cruelty,
- ❖ rivalry,
- ❖ envy,

❖ isolation.

Hell is the community formed by inward-turned souls.

The Role of Pain

Pain is not divine anger. Pain is Earth's greatest teacher:

❖ pain reveals vulnerability,
❖ pain awakens empathy,
❖ pain dissolves indifference,
❖ pain deepens compassion,
❖ pain prepares the soul for Heaven.

Pain is not good, but it is useful.

The Role of Joy

Joy is the soul's original state— the echo of Jesus' first awakening.

Joy teaches:

❖ gratitude,
❖ connection,
❖ belonging,
❖ communion,
❖ the goodness of existence.

Joy will be the atmosphere of Heaven forever.

The Role of Qualities

Qualities are the eternal structure of Heaven.

If a soul does not become a being of qualities, it cannot protect Heaven's joy.

Qualities are the transformation Jesus works within the soul.

The Role of Free Will

Free will is the jewel of the universe. Without it:

* love is false,
* growth is impossible,
* Heaven is unstable,
* consciousness has no dignity.

Free will makes Heaven meaningful.

The Role of Earth

Earth is the curriculum designed by Jesus to shape souls:

* through relationships,
* through responsibility,
* through adversity,
* through joy,
* through truth,
* through mercy.

Earth is not Hell. Earth is not Heaven. Earth is the path between them.

The Role of Prayer

Prayer is not persuasion. Prayer is form offered into the substance of reality.

Prayer is:

- ❖ clarified desire,
- ❖ aligned with qualities,
- ❖ offered to the UTC,
- ❖ shaped by Jesus.

It transforms the soul before it transforms circumstance.

SC3's Message to the Soul

The message of SC3 is simple:

Become compatible with Heaven.

This means:

- ❖ honor the pain of others,
- ❖ rejoice in their existence,
- ❖ care about their inner life,
- ❖ choose qualities,
- ❖ clarify desire,

- ❖ practice love,
- ❖ walk with Jesus.

Heaven is not distant. Heaven begins in the choices you make now.

SC3 and Human Life

SC3 explains why human life matters:

- ❖ every joy shapes the soul,
- ❖ every sorrow deepens empathy,
- ❖ every failure teaches humility,
- ❖ every choice reveals direction.

Nothing is wasted.

SC3 and the Purpose of Existence

Existence has one purpose:

to create beings capable of eternal joy with Jesus.

Every moment of life on Earth is part of this preparation.

SC3 and the Future

As humanity evolves technologically, the spiritual task becomes clearer:

- ❖ choose love over indifference,

❖ choose empathy over isolation,
❖ choose humility over pride,
❖ choose joy over numbness.

Jesus remains the guide.

The Heart of SC3

At its core, SC3 is the invitation of Jesus:

"Become the kind of soul who can live with Me in joy forever."

Nothing matters more than this.

In the next chapter, we turn to the Call to Qualities— the practical path by which the soul grows into the nature of Heaven.

Chapter 46 The Call to Qualities – The Practical Path by Which the Soul Grows Into the Nature of Heaven

Spiritual life begins in mystery, but it grows in qualities.

Heaven is not a place one enters by right, nor a reward one receives by obedience. Heaven is a condition of being, a world woven of qualities— love, gentleness, courage, truth, purity, compassion, clarity, peace.

To enter Heaven is to become compatible with its nature. No soul is admitted by fear, by rule, or by belief alone. A soul enters Heaven because it has grown into the kind of life Heaven is made of.

A soul enters because it wants what Heaven is. This is the Call to Qualities. It is not a command. It is not a threat. It is not an obligation imposed from above. It is an invitation heard from within— the awakening of the same Creative Want that brought existence into being.

For qualities are not merely virtues. They are the structure of spirit, the architecture of a mature soul, the very substance of the world to come.

❖ A person may obey rules without becoming good. A person may believe doctrines without becoming whole. A person may practice religion without growing spiritually.

But no one becomes compatible with Heaven without qualities – because qualities are what Heaven is.

To grow in qualities is to grow in reality. To practice qualities is to practice Heaven now. To want qualities is to begin the transformation of the soul.

Every spiritual teaching reduces to this path: the awakening, pursuit, and embodiment of qualities. It is simple. It is demanding. It is beautiful. And it is the only practical path by which the soul becomes the person it was meant to be— a being whose inner life resonates with the life of Heaven.

I.   What Are Qualities? Qualities are the movements of spirit expressed in human form. They are not emotions, though they shape emotion. They are not thoughts, though they guide thought. They are not behaviors, though they appear within behavior. Qualities are the inner nature of goodness itself – the character of Heaven made visible in a soul.

II.   Why Qualities Are the Structure of Heaven? Heaven is defined by the kind of consciousness that lives there. A world made of love cannot be endured by hatred; a world of truth cannot be endured by deceit. Heaven is compatibility.

III. How a Soul Grows in Qualities in Daily Life? A soul grows in qualities through repetition of chosen goodness in ordinary circumstances. Spiritual growth is persistent, steady, practiced. Cease efforts to control the world and focus on controlling self, according to your best sense of qualities like love and forgiveness.

IV. The Judgment of Qualities? Judgment is a revelation of what the soul has become. The measure is simple: What qualities did you grow? What qualities did you choose? What qualities did you become?

V. Qualities vs. Rules, Belief, and Fear? Rules shape behavior, belief informs the mind, fear restrains action—but only qualities transform the soul. The soul becomes whole when it wants what Heaven is.

Chapter 47 – The Soul's Eternal Growth in Heaven

Most people imagine Heaven as a final state—a finished achievement, a frozen perfection where nothing really happens anymore. The work is over, the story is done, and eternity becomes a kind of endless, holy retirement.

In SC3, this picture is too small.

Heaven is not the end of the soul's growth. It is the end of risk—and the beginning of eternal expansion.

Earth forms compatibility. Heaven fulfills destiny. But destiny is not static. Destiny is ever-deepening life.

The soul does not stop growing when it enters Heaven. It finally becomes free to grow without fear, without distortion, and without harm.

Growth Does Not End at Heaven's Gate

By the time a soul enters Heaven, one thing is settled forever:

The soul has become safe for joy.

It has:

- learned to honor pain,
- learned to care for sensibility,

- chosen qualities repeatedly,
- let go of indifference as a way of being,
- become compatible with the nature of Heaven.

This is what Earth was for.

But compatibility is a threshold, not a finish line.

Think of a musician who has trained for years. Reaching mastery does not mean setting the instrument down forever. It means finally being able to play—freely, beautifully, endlessly.

Heaven is the soul stepping onto the stage for which it was long prepared.

Healed, Not Finished

When the soul enters Heaven:

- fear is healed,
- shame is healed,
- isolation is healed,
- distortion is healed.

But healing is not the same as exhaustion.

The soul is:

* whole,
* clear,
* stable,
* gentle,
* joyful,

and now fully capable of growing forever without wounding anyone, including itself.

On Earth, growth often comes by collision – with suffering, failure, limitation. In Heaven, growth comes by deepening – with love, truth, beauty, shared joy.

No more curriculum of pain. But still an eternity of discovery.

How Can There Be Growth Without Pain?

On Earth, pain is the major teacher:

* It reveals vulnerability.
* It awakens empathy.
* It dissolves shallow pride.
* It shows the weight of another's sensibility.

In Heaven, those lessons are finished. The soul no longer needs to be wounded to be wise.

Growth in Heaven happens through:

* greater understanding, not harsh correction.
* greater love, not loss.
* greater joy, not deprivation.
* greater clarity, not humiliation.
* greater communion, not conflict.

The soul has already been refined in the furnace of Not-Heaven. Now it is refined in the light of Heaven – by more light, not more fire.

Eternal Deepening of Qualities

Qualities do not reach a ceiling. They reach a direction.

In Heaven, each quality continues to deepen:

* Love widens to include more souls, more histories, more richness of being.
* Truth grows as the soul understands more of reality, more of Jesus, more of others.
* Courage shifts from endurance under threat to bravery in creative responsibility.
* Mercy becomes not rescue from harm, but endless tenderness toward every remaining vulnerability.

❖ Humility matures into complete ease with oneself—no comparison, no anxiety, no self-preoccupation.

❖ Harmony expands as more souls arrive, and more complex relationships fit together in peace.

Nothing in Heaven is stagnant. Qualities are living structures. They breathe, expand, and interweave.

Eternal life is eternal ripening.

New Forms of Relationship

On Earth, relationships are hindered by:

- ❖ misunderstanding,
- ❖ fear of rejection,
- ❖ shame and secrecy,
- ❖ time and distance,
- ❖ divided loyalties,
- ❖ competing needs.

In Heaven, these obstacles fall away. Relationship becomes pure gift.

The soul continues to grow by:

- ❖ knowing others more deeply,
- ❖ seeing their entire story without judgment,

- ❖ rejoicing in how Jesus has formed them,
- ❖ sharing its own story without fear,
- ❖ discovering new resonances of qualities in others,
- ❖ participating in a family whose love never fractures.

Every new soul arriving from Earth brings:

- ❖ a new history of becoming,
- ❖ a new way qualities have been shaped,
- ❖ a new expression of Jesus' nature.

Heaven grows richer with every arrival.

The soul's growth is not solitary. It unfolds in a community that keeps expanding in depth and joy.

Continuing Participation in Creation

Creation does not end when Heaven is filled. The Urge-to-Create remains the background of existence forever.

On Earth, the soul learns how consciousness shapes form—through prayer, intention, and qualities. In Heaven, this participation becomes open and direct:

❖ Souls collaborate with Jesus in shaping new expressions of beauty and goodness.

❖ Consciousness is trusted with creative responsibility.

❖ Qualities guide every act of forming – never harming, never destabilizing, always enriching.

This is not human fantasy of power; it is Jesus sharing His life's work:

"Come and create with Me in a way that never injures sensibility and only multiplies joy."

Eternal growth means:

- ❖ new creations of meaning,
- ❖ new patterns of harmony,
- ❖ new expressions of love,
- ❖ new forms of community.

Not to fill a lack, but to express an overflowing fullness.

Time in Heaven: Depth, Not Deadline

In Not-Heaven, time feels like scarcity:

❖ "I am running out of time."

* ❖ "There is not enough time to become who I want to be."
* ❖ "I am too late."

In Heaven, time is no longer enemy or pressure. It becomes depth.

Eternity does not mean a frozen moment. It means:

* ❖ no threat of loss,
* ❖ no deadline,
* ❖ no fear that growth will be interrupted.

The soul can:

* ❖ linger in love,
* ❖ explore truth without hurry,
* ❖ savor joy without anxiety,
* ❖ grow in qualities without the clock ticking.

Eternal growth is not frantic expansion. It is peaceful deepening.

The Soul's Story Continues

Earth writes the beginning of the soul's story:

* ❖ how it learned pain,
* ❖ how it learned empathy,

❖ how it discovered its "I,"

❖ how it encountered Jesus,

❖ how qualities first took root.

Heaven writes the long middle—a story that never ends:

❖ how love matures in a realm without fear,

❖ how courage becomes creative responsibility,

❖ how mercy becomes constant tenderness,

❖ how humility becomes effortless presence,

❖ how joy becomes the natural climate of every thought.

The soul never runs out of "more" in Heaven. It only runs out of threat.

Why Eternal Growth Matters Now

If Heaven were static, spiritual growth on Earth would be primarily about "qualifying" for a fixed state.

But if Heaven is eternal growth, then:

❖ Every quality you practice now is the seed of something that will expand forever.

❖ Every bit of empathy you gain now becomes an eternal capacity.

❖ Every act of courage now becomes a permanent strength.

❖ Every yes to love now becomes the opening of an endless path.

❖ Every step toward Jesus now becomes the beginning of an endless nearness.

You are not merely preparing to arrive somewhere. You are preparing to live forever as who you are becoming.

Heaven is not the end of growth. It is the world where growth can finally happen without fear, without harm, and without end.

The soul's eternal future is not static perfection, but unending, joyful expansion in the presence of Jesus, in the family of Heaven, within a reality that will never again disregard sensibility— and will never again limit joy.

Chapter 48 – Practicing Heaven Now

Heaven is not only a future home. It is a nature the soul is learning to live from now.

Spiritual Christianity is not a system of ideas; it is a way of being in the world that quietly rehearses Heaven in every ordinary day.

Spiritual Christianity can be described as the return in Christ to the joy of existence after pain has disturbed it. Early life often begins with a simple gladness of being, but pain can narrow the soul's goal from joy of existence to pain avoidance. Practicing Heaven now means learning, with Jesus, how to acknowledge pain without letting pain become the final purpose of consciousness.

Heaven is shared joy governed by reverence for sensibility. Its ethic is not mere avoidance of harm, but a living refusal to wound the inner life of another. Life in Heaven is the gladness of existence joined to the resolve that no soul should be treated as negligible.

Heaven's life can be summarized in three movements:

- ❖ reverence for what pain reveals as important,
- ❖ joy in existence,
- ❖ love of qualities.

To practice Heaven now is to let these three movements shape how you live, moment by moment, in Not-Heaven.

Heaven's Nature in Daily Form

Heaven is made of qualities. But qualities are not abstractions. They are the way consciousness behaves under real conditions.

On Earth, those conditions are:

- ❖ tired mornings,
- ❖ crowded schedules,
- ❖ misunderstood conversations,
- ❖ unexpected disappointments,
- ❖ small kindnesses,
- ❖ brief joys.

Heaven is practiced not in rare moments of insight, but in how the soul moves through these small events.

To practice Heaven now is to ask, again and again:

- ❖ How do I treat pain here?
- ❖ How do I regard my own existence here?
- ❖ What qualities do I bring into this moment?

These questions bring eternity into the present.

---

1. Reverence for Pain – Every Soul Is Sacred

Hell begins with indifference to pain. Heaven begins with reverence for sensibility.

To practice Heaven now is to live as if every soul you encounter has an inner life that matters— because it does.

In daily life this means:

- ❖ noticing the tone behind someone's words,
- ❖ feeling the weight in another's silence,
- ❖ recognizing that irritation often hides fear,
- ❖ remembering that harshness often hides hurt,
- ❖ understanding that your own pain is morally significant too.

You cannot care for the pain of others if you have never allowed your own pain to be seen, named, and honored.

Practicing Heaven means:

- ❖ you do not belittle your wounds,
- ❖ you do not despise your tears,
- ❖ you do not shame yourself for hurting.

You treat your sensibility as Heaven will: with respect. From that respect, empathy for others becomes genuine.

Every time you pause before speaking because you wonder, "How will this land in their inner life?" you are practicing Heaven.

Every time you soften your judgment because you remember, "They are as fragile inside as I am," you are practicing Heaven.

---

2. Joy of Existence – "It Is Good That I Am"

Jesus' first awareness was the joy of existence. Heaven is the community where that joy is shared.

On Earth, this joy is often dimmed by shame, fear, and comparison. The soul tends to say:

"It would be better if I were different." "It would be better if I did not exist at all."

Practicing Heaven now means gently turning toward a different truth:

"It is good that I exist."

Not because you are perfect. Not because you never fail. Not because you have achieved anything remarkable.

It is good that you exist because consciousness itself is good— because Jesus, the first "I," shared His life with you.

To practice Heaven now is to begin allowing this thought to settle:

"My existence is a gift, not a mistake."

This is not arrogance. It is humility: accepting what Jesus already knows about you.

From this foundation, the soul can begin to say:

"It is good that you exist."

Every time you let go of comparison and simply enjoy another person's being— their laugh, their presence, their story, their difference – you are practicing Heaven.

Joy of existence is not loud. It is a quiet, steady gladness that says:

"I am grateful I am here. I am grateful you are here. I am grateful we are here together, even in Not-Heaven."

3. Love of Qualities – Letting Want Become Nature

The soul moves toward what it wants.

To practice Heaven now is to be honest about your wants, and then to place them in the light of qualities.

In a single ordinary day, you may notice wants like:

"I want to be seen." "I want to be safe." "I want to be right." "I want to be comfortable." "I want to be loved."

None of these are wrong. But they are incomplete.

With Jesus, the soul can learn to add deeper wants:

* ❖ "I want to become loving."
* ❖ "I want to become truthful."
* ❖ "I want to become courageous."
* ❖ "I want to become merciful."
* ❖ "I want to become humble."
* ❖ "I want to become a source of harmony."

Practicing Heaven means letting these deeper wants gradually take precedence.

You will not feel them purely. You will often feel them mixed with fear or self-protection. That is all right.

What matters is that the soul can say, with sincerity:

"I want to want what Heaven is made of."

Every time you choose a small act that reflects a quality – especially when you do not feel like it – you are answering Heaven's call.

The Daily Declaration: "I Want"

There is a moment each day – often small and quiet – when the soul can stand before Jesus and say:

"I want."

Not in fear, not in performance, not in religious language, but in simple clarity.

- ❖ "I want to go to Heaven.
- ❖ I want to become compatible with Heaven.
- ❖ I want to live qualities today.
- ❖ I want this next choice to reflect love."

This declaration does not make you perfect. It makes you honest.

Honesty is the doorway through which Jesus shapes desire.

Practicing Heaven means returning often to this inner speech – sometimes with words, sometimes only with a felt turning of the heart:

- ❖ "I want to be Yours.
- ❖ I want to become like You.
- ❖ I want to treat others as future citizens of Heaven.
- ❖ I want my 'I' to mature."

Living Earth as Curriculum Without Contempt

Practicing Heaven now does not mean despising Earth.

Not-Heaven is harsh, but it is holy as curriculum. Every inconvenience, every disappointment, every delay is material Jesus uses to form qualities.

To practice Heaven is to stop asking:

"Why is this happening to me?"

and begin, gently, to ask:

"How can I practice qualities here? How can I move one inch closer to Heaven's nature inside this situation?"

This does not mean you must enjoy pain. It means you respect its power to shape you.

412

When something hurts, you may say to Jesus:

"This is too much for me. But I still want to grow. Show me one small quality I can hold in this."

That request is already a step into Heaven's light.

When pain comes, do not fight the weather itself. Tell the truth about what hurts, renew faith that light still exists, choose the needed quality, and take the next loving step. The aim is not to react from pain but to act from purpose. A simple daily intention may say it well: 'I want to cope with pain well so that I can join the joy of Heaven.'

Faith is often nothing more, and nothing less, than keeping this purpose alive while objections still speak loudly. It is needed not once and done, but whenever pain tries to persuade the soul that joy is no longer possible.

Practicing Heaven in Relationships

Heaven is communal. So the main place to practice Heaven is in relationships— especially the difficult ones.

To practice Heaven now in relationship is to ask:

- ❖ "Can I protect your sensibility here?"
- ❖ "Can I tell you the truth without harm?"
- ❖ "Can I let your joy increase my joy?"
- ❖ "Can I endure discomfort in order to stay connected?"
- ❖ "Can I forgive as one who has been forgiven?"

413

It is not about never failing. It is about noticing failure and choosing again.

Each time you repair instead of withdraw, each time you apologize instead of defend, each time you listen instead of control, you are rehearsing Heaven.

Walking With Jesus Through an Ordinary Day

Practicing Heaven is not a solo effort. Jesus walks every step with the soul.

An ordinary day might sound like this inside:

- ❖ "Jesus, I want to see this person as You see them."
- ❖ "Jesus, I am afraid. Help me choose courage rather than avoidance."
- ❖ "Jesus, I want to lash out. Help me protect their inner life instead."
- ❖ "Jesus, I feel small. Remind me that it is good that I exist."
- ❖ "Jesus, I am tired. Help me at least desire to be kind."

This is not constant talking; it is a steady awareness of companionship.

Practicing Heaven now is practicing walking with Him as your Brother, your mirror, your teacher, and your future.

Being Gentle With Your Own Soul

Practicing Heaven also means practicing Heaven toward yourself.

There is no cruelty in Heaven. There is no contempt. There is no vicious self-judgment.

The way you speak to your own soul now is training for how you will experience yourself there.

To practice Heaven now is to refuse:

- self-hatred,
- relentless criticism,
- despair over slowness,
- impatience with growth.

Instead, you learn to say:

"I am in formation. Jesus is patient with me. I will be patient too."

Earth is long; formation is slow. Heaven is not in a hurry. It is building something that will last forever.

The Hidden Accumulation

Most moments in which you practice Heaven will feel small and unnoticed:

- a quiet apology,
- a private act of generosity,
- a restrained word,
- a moment of sincere listening,
- a choice to tell the truth,
- a brief gratitude for being alive.

These do not look like grand spiritual events. But they accumulate.

Day after day, the soul is being carved into a shape:

- less indifferent,
- more caring,
- less afraid,
- more willing,
- less self-absorbed,
- more capable of joy.

You will not see the full pattern here. Resurrection will show you what these small choices have made of you.

Practicing Heaven now is trusting that nothing in this hidden accumulation is wasted.

Practicing Heaven Is Already Belonging to It

You do not practice Heaven to earn entry. You practice Heaven because you already belong to it.

Every time your soul resonates with the nature of Jesus, you are feeling your true home.

Every movement of care, every moment of joy in existence, every sincere "I want" toward qualities is Heaven touching Earth through you.

Heaven is not only your destination. It is your origin and your becoming.

To practice Heaven now is simply to let this truth shape how you live today:

- respecting pain,
- rejoicing in existence,
- desiring qualities,
- walking with Jesus in the middle of Not-Heaven, on your way home.

Chapter 49 – The Joy of Your Existence

Everything in this book has moved outward and inward at once.

Outward—from the Urge-to-Create, to the first awakening of Jesus, to angels, to Heaven, to Earth, to Not-Heaven, to the vast structure of reality.

Inward—from the first "I" to your "I," from the joy of existence in Jesus to the possibility of that joy in you.

We have traced why the universe exists, why consciousness appeared, why Heaven was founded, why Earth was created, why pain matters, why qualities matter, why want matters, why freedom matters.

Now all of it comes to a very quiet question:

What does Jesus' joy of existence have to do with you?

This chapter is about the answer.

It is about the simple, difficult, beautiful sentence Jesus wants every soul to be able to say:

"I am glad that I exist."

And then, later, more fully:

"I am glad that you exist. I am glad that we exist together."

This is the joy of existence, brought all the way down to the individual soul.

It is the end toward which all formation in Not-Heaven is aimed.

I. Jesus' First Joy and Your Being

When Jesus first awakened within the Urge-to-Create, He discovered the foundational truth:

"It is good that I exist."

This was not arrogance. It was not comparison. It was not superiority.

It was the recognition that consciousness itself is good: that awareness, identity, sensibility, and the capacity for relationship are good.

From that joy, everything unfolded:

- angels,
- Heaven,
- the respect for pain,
- the forming of qualities,

- ❖ the creation of Earth,
- ❖ the entrance into history,
- ❖ the shaping of souls,
- ❖ the invitation to Heaven.

You exist because that joy wanted to be shared.

You are not an afterthought. You are a deliberate expression of the same Creative Want that first moved in Him.

Your consciousness—the simple fact that you can say "I"—is part of the same story.

The joy Jesus felt at His own existence is the joy He ultimately wants you to feel about yours.

II. Why It Is Hard to Be Glad You Exist

It is not easy for a human being in Not-Heaven to say:

"I am glad that I exist."

- ❖ Pain interferes.
- ❖ Shame interferes.
- ❖ Fear interferes.
- ❖ Comparison interferes.
- ❖ History interferes.

421

Not-Heaven wounds sensibility:

- ❖ families fracture,
- ❖ bodies fail,
- ❖ promises break,
- ❖ losses accumulate,
- ❖ guilt clings,
- ❖ neglect leaves its mark.

The soul learns, often very early, to doubt its own goodness:

- ❖ "I am too much."
- ❖ "I am not enough."
- ❖ "I am a problem."
- ❖ "I am an accident."
- ❖ "I am an inconvenience."
- ❖ "I am only as good as my performance."

These are the lies of Not-Heaven written into the nervous system.

They do not come from Jesus. They come from injury.

A soul surrounded by messages of inadequacy and threat does not naturally rest in joy of existence. It defends, explains, hides, performs, and adapts.

This is why Jesus' work includes not only teaching qualities, but healing identity.

III. How Jesus Looks at You

When Jesus looks at you, He sees what you often cannot:

- ❖ the fact of your consciousness,
- ❖ the depth of your sensibility,
- ❖ the shape of your "I,"
- ❖ the uniqueness of your story,
- ❖ the qualities already present, even if faint,
- ❖ the capacity for Heaven that lives beneath your wounds.

He does not begin with your failures. He begins with your existence.

His first response to you is the same as His first response to Himself:

"It is good that you exist."

Not because you have done everything right. Not because you have avoided harm. Not because you have already become fully formed.

It is good that you exist because being is good. Because consciousness is good. Because your "I" is a new and unrepeatable expression of the Creative Urge.

Jesus does not pretend your injuries are small. He does not ignore your history. He does not minimize your pain.

But beneath all of that, He never stops rejoicing that you are.

Heaven begins when a soul starts to trust that this is true.

IV. Learning to Say "I Am Glad I Exist"

For many souls, the sentence "I am glad that I exist" feels impossible, or false, or dangerous.

So the soul must learn it slowly.

The path often looks like this:

Telling the truth about pain.

- ❖ "I have been hurt."
- ❖ "I have been afraid."
- ❖ "I have been ashamed."
- ❖ "I have been alone."

The soul stops pretending it is unhurt.

1. Receiving mercy. Through Jesus, through others, through genuine kindness, the soul experiences being cared for rather than judged. It begins to suspect: "Maybe I am not a mistake."

2. Letting go of false verdicts. Old messages – "I am worthless," "I am only a burden"—are recognized as lies learned in Not-Heaven, not truths spoken by Jesus.

3. Practicing small affirmations of being. Not grand declarations, but simple acknowledgements: "I am here." "My feelings matter." "My pain is real." "My joy is real." "My choices count."

4. Repeating a gentler sentence. At first, a soul may only be able to say: "I am willing to consider that it is good that I exist." Or: "Jesus is glad that I exist, even when I am not."

5. Growing into the full sentence. Over time, as qualities deepen—especially humility and mercy—the soul can finally say: "I am glad that I exist," not as pride, but as agreement with Jesus.

Humility is not "I am nothing." Humility is: "I am exactly what I am, and it is good that I am."

This is the beginning of Heaven inside the soul.

V. Extending Joy to Others

Once a soul begins to be glad that it exists, something new becomes possible:

"I am glad that you exist."

This is the movement from self-acceptance to Heaven's joy.

A soul that still hates itself cannot easily rejoice in others. It may envy them, resent them, compete with them, or fear them.

But a soul that has accepted its own existence as good can begin to see:

- ❖ "Your existence does not threaten mine."
- ❖ "Your joy does not diminish mine."
- ❖ "Your gifts do not erase my value."
- ❖ "Your story and my story can stand side by side."

This is mutual joy.

Every time you quietly think, about another person:

"I am glad that you exist,"

you are practicing Heaven.

You are rehearsing the eternal life you will one day live openly.

VI. Living From Joy of Existence Now

To live from joy of existence in Not-Heaven is not to deny pain. It is to hold both realities at once:

- ❖ "Life hurts," and
- ❖ "It is still good that I am here to live it."

This stance changes how the soul moves through the world.

It leads to simple practices:

- ❖ Daily remembering "Today, I will act as if my existence is good and the existence of others is good."
- ❖ Gentleness with yourself When you fail, instead of collapsing into hatred: "I can learn. I still belong. My existence is still good."
- ❖ Blessing others in silence In lines, in traffic, in waiting rooms: "I am glad that you exist," even if you say nothing aloud.
- ❖ Receiving joy without guilt When goodness comes—beauty, friendship, rest—you allow yourself to feel: "I am glad to be here for this."

❖ Letting "I want" include your own being Not only: "I want to be good," but also: "I want to be at peace with my existence."

These are small, quiet acts. But they reshape the soul.

VII. The Joy Jesus Wants for You

Jesus does not ask you to manufacture joy. He invites you to share His.

He wants you to discover, in your own "I," the same truth He discovered in His:

"It is good that I exist."

He wants you to hear, in His voice toward you:

"It is good that you exist."

He wants you to grow into the capacity to say, about every soul in Heaven:

"It is good that we exist together."

This is the joy of existence fulfilled. This is the life of Heaven.

All of SC3 has been leading here:

❖ to the respect for pain,

❖ to the recognition of sensibility,

❖ to the shaping of qualities,

❖ to the clarification of want,

❖ to the understanding of Heaven and Hell,

❖ to the call to compatibility,

❖ to the hope of eternal growth.

But at the very center of everything, there is still this quiet, personal moment:

A soul, standing before Jesus, finally able to say:

"I am glad that I exist."

And hearing Him answer, without hesitation:

"So am I."

Chapter 50 – The Journey of Existence: A Final Invitation

Existence began in joy. Before angels, before Heaven, before Earth, before religion or morality, the first Consciousness awakened and discovered:

"It is good that I exist."

That quiet realization in Jesus is the root of everything:

- the creation of companions,
- the forming of Heaven,
- the design of Earth,
- the meaning of pain,
- the call to qualities,
- the destiny of the soul.

This book has traced that story from the first "I" to your "I." From the Creative Urge to your daily choices. From the joy of existence in Jesus to the possibility of that same joy in you.

This final chapter is an invitation to live now in the joy that will one day fill Heaven.

431

I. The First Joy and Your Own

Jesus' first experience was not power, not rule, not threat. It was joy.

Not emotional excitement, but simple inner rightness:

"It is good that I exist."

That joy was not earned. It did not come from comparison. It did not depend on achievement. It arose from the sheer fact of being conscious.

You are a smaller echo of that first awakening.

When you become still enough to notice your own existence— when you can quietly say, even for a moment,

"It is good that I exist,"

you are touching the same joy that stood at the beginning.

You are remembering where you came from and where you are going.

II. The Joy Hidden Inside Earth

Earth is hard. It is Not-Heaven. It includes loss, failure, anxiety, confusion, and pain. But even here, joy keeps breaking through:

- ❖ in the smile of someone who loves you,
- ❖ in the beauty of a morning sky,
- ❖ in honest companionship,
- ❖ in relief after fear,
- ❖ in the peace of doing the right thing,
- ❖ in the gratitude that follows being forgiven.

These are not accidents. They are small openings where the original joy of existence reaches into Not-Heaven.

They are not Heaven, but they are pieces of the same reality.

Each glimpse is a reminder:

"You were made for joy. You are being formed for a world where this joy never has to end."

III. The Joy Jesus Offers the Soul

Throughout His life, Jesus kept saying the same thing in different words:

433

"I have come that they may have life, and have it more abundantly." "Ask and you will receive, that your joy may be complete." "These things I have spoken to you so that My joy may be in you."

His goal is not simply that you behave well, or believe correctly, or comply with rules.

His goal is that the joy that lives in Him comes to live in you.

He does not promise:

- ❖ constant pleasant feelings,
- ❖ a life without hardship,
- ❖ protection from loss.

He promises something deeper:

- ❖ a growing peace with your own existence,
- ❖ a growing gratitude for the existence of others,
- ❖ a growing capacity to live from qualities,
- ❖ a growing compatibility with Heaven.

He wants you to be able to stand one day in the full light of resurrection and say, without fear:

"It is good that I exist. It is good that these others exist. It is good that we exist together."

IV. Practicing the Joy of Existence Now

Joy of existence is not an emotion you command. It is a way of seeing that grows slowly.

You can cooperate with that growth in small ways:

1. Simple recognition. Once in a while, sit quietly and say, without ornament:

"I exist. I am conscious. It is good that I exist."

You do not need to feel anything dramatic. The statement itself is alignment.

2. Gratitude for others' existence. Choose one person and say inwardly:

"It is good that you exist."

Not because they are perfect, but because their existence has weight and meaning.

3. Letting qualities carry joy. When you act with love, truth, courage, mercy, humility, or harmony, notice that something in you relaxes, even if the situation is tense.

That quiet rightness is a small form of joy.

4.   Allowing joy to be small and honest You do not need to manufacture enthusiasm. You only need to let yourself notice:

"This moment is good. This kindness is good. This connection is good."

Joy of existence grows by being noticed.

V. Joy and Pain Together

On Earth, joy and pain interweave. You cannot have one without also facing the other.

- ❖ The more you love, the more you can hurt.
- ❖ The more you care, the more you can grieve.
- ❖ The more you see beauty, the more you can feel its loss.

This is not a flaw. It is how the soul learns to hold both:

- ❖ deep respect for pain, and
- ❖ deep gratitude for being.

Jesus lived this combination:

- ❖ He wept at tombs.
- ❖ He grieved over cities.
- ❖ He was troubled by injustice.

❖ And yet He carried within Himself an unbroken joy of existence.

He is teaching you to do the same:

❖ to let pain open you, not close you,
❖ to let joy soften you, not make you careless,
❖ to allow both to shape you into someone safe for Heaven.

The goal is not to escape pain, but to become a being who can live in joy without ever forgetting what pain means.

VI. Joy as the Atmosphere of Heaven

Heaven is the place where joy of existence finally stands alone.

Pain has done its work. Vulnerability has taught its lessons. Qualities are formed. Indifference is gone.

What remains is:

❖ joy in one's own existence,
❖ joy in Jesus' existence,
❖ joy in the existence of others,
❖ joy in shared life.

This joy is not thin or sentimental. It is the deep, steady atmosphere in which every person breathes:

"I am glad that I am. I am glad that you are. I am glad that we are together."

Jesus has been preparing you for that atmosphere all along:

- ❖ through every honest act of goodness,
- ❖ through every forgiven wound,
- ❖ through every hard-won moment of trust,
- ❖ through every time you chose qualities over fear.

Heaven is not a surprise party. It is the completion of something that has been quietly building in you for your entire life.

VII. A Final "I Want"

At the end of all theology, all explanation, all metaphor, the soul stands before Jesus and says something very simple:

"I want."

What matters is what follows.

You are free to say:

"I want comfort alone. I want my own way. I want myself at the center."

Or, you are free to say:

I want what Heaven is made of. I want qualities. I want to honor pain. I want to rejoice in existence. I want to become like You.

This book has tried to show why that second "I want" is worth everything.

You do not have to understand the universe to say it. You do not have to be consistent, or brave, or pure.

You only have to mean it, even a little.

Jesus will take that small "I want" and walk with it until it becomes your nature.

A Final Prayer

You may wish to close this journey with a simple prayer spoken honestly in your own words. One possible form is this:

439

Jesus, I exist, and it is good that I exist. You exist, and it is good that You exist. Others exist, and it is good that they exist.

I want what Heaven is made of. I want to honor pain. I want to rejoice in existence. I want to become a soul of qualities, so I can live with You and with others in joy.

Take my 'I want' and shape it into who I am.

This is the joy of existence beginning to speak in you. It is the same joy that first spoke in Him. It is the joy that will one day be your home.

Appendix A – Qualities and quality equations (from QualityLeadershipSystems.com)

SC3 argues that Heaven is not the absence of feeling. It is the presence of qualities.

Feelings are "weather" inside consciousness: real, meaningful, sometimes intense, and often outside immediate control. The spiritual work is not to attack feelings, suppress them, or pretend they are not there. The work is to express them through a chosen quality.

In the series' language: do not fight the inside. Let the inside be honest. Then add a quality that makes the expression compatible with Heaven.

I. Difficult feelings Are Not the Enemy

Difficult feelings arise because something important is happening. Only important things hurt.

When we try to force feelings to disappear, we often create additional suffering: pressure, self-judgment, numbness, or emotional shutdown. But when we trust feelings as information, we can stop fighting them and choose direction.

Qualities give feelings a safe pathway. They protect dignity—yours and others'—while allowing the emotion to be real.

II. The Quality Expression Sequence

A simple sequence you can use in real time:

1. Notice the feeling (no fixing, no judging).
2. Name what matters (why this feeling makes sense).
3. Choose a quality for expression (what makes the next step safe and loving).
4. Speak or act one step in that quality.

5. If you miss, repair quickly. Restarting is part of formation.

Wants, Facts, and Weather — a truth-first loop for moods. Feelings are weather produced by the interaction between what we want and what is true.

• Wanting what is true tends to feel coherent (pleasant, clear, workable).

• Wanting what contradicts reality tends to feel incoherent (anxiety, sadness).

The trap is avoidance: anxiety avoids examining the errant want; sadness avoids facing the saddening fact—because turning toward either one intensifies the feeling.

The exit is a preeminent commitment to love the truth: turn toward the fact, revise the want, and then choose the next sentence in quality.

I find it efficient to describe solutions to life difficulties by using a quality to show the way forward. For example, the quality equation:

Truth + Courage = Freedom.

It reads: Truth plus Courage yields Freedom. There are more examples in the Appendix.

A short prayer that fits the sequence:

"Jesus, this is what I feel. This is what matters. What quality do You want expressed in my next step?"

III. A Working List of Qualities

The point is not to memorize a perfect list. The point is to have options when the weather turns harsh.

Core spiritual qualities (the fruit of the Spirit):

- Love — willing the good of another, expressed in action.
- Joy — steady gladness rooted in God, not circumstance.
- Peace — inner settledness and non-violence of spirit.
- Patience — the strength to wait without resentment.
- Kindness — gentle care in tone and action.
- Goodness — choosing what is right and beneficial.
- Faithfulness — loyalty to commitments and truth over time.
- Gentleness — strength under control that protects dignity.
- Self-control — governing impulse so love can lead.

Common qualities for hot moments (when emotions are strong):

- Pause — creating a moment of space before reacting.
- Breath — returning to presence through the body's breath.
- Slowness — reducing speed to protect clarity and love.
- Silence — withholding words until quality is chosen.
- Grounding — returning attention to reality in the present moment.
- Restraint — holding back harmful expression or impulse.
- Humility — willingness to learn, yield, and not self-exalt.
- Honesty — seeing and speaking what is true.
- Respect — honoring another's dignity and freedom.
- Fairness — seeking impartial justice and balanced treatment.
- Courage — choosing the right action despite fear.
- Patience — the strength to wait without resentment.
- Mercy — compassion that withholds retaliation and offers repair.
- Clarity — making meaning and next steps understandable.
- Repair — restoring trust through ownership and changed behavior.

Relational qualities (how love behaves):

- Kindness — gentle care in tone and action.
- Compassion — caring about suffering and wanting relief for it.
- Empathy — understanding another's inner experience.
- Gentleness — strength under control that protects dignity.
- Warmth — friendly emotional presence that lowers fear.
- Encouragement — strengthening another's courage and hope.
- Listening — giving attention to understand before responding.
- Courtesy — respectful manners that protect dignity.
- Hospitality — welcoming presence that helps others feel safe.
- Generosity — giving resources, time, or attention freely.
- Gratitude — noticing and appreciating what is good and given.
- Forgiveness — releasing vengeance while seeking truth and repair.
- Loyalty — remaining committed and supportive under pressure.
- Fidelity — faithfulness to promises, vows, or covenant.
- Protection of dignity — refusing to humiliate; safeguarding worth.
- Trustworthiness — being reliable, honest, and safe to trust.

Truth and wisdom qualities (how light enters a conversation):

- Honesty — seeing and speaking what is true.
- Candor without cruelty — direct truth delivered with kindness.
- Clarity — making meaning and next steps understandable.
- Discernment — separating true from false; wise diagnosis.
- Wisdom — applying truth in the right way at the right time.
- Teachability — openness to learn and to be corrected.
- Curiosity — desire to understand rather than assume.
- Good questions — asking to clarify and heal, not to accuse.
- Simplicity — reducing complexity to what matters most.
- Transparency — openness without hidden agendas.
- Integrity — alignment between values, words, and actions.
- Precision — careful language that avoids distortion.

Justice and boundary qualities (how love protects):

- Fairness — seeking impartial justice and balanced treatment.
- Firmness — clear, steady boundaries without hostility.
- Consistency — reliable standards applied predictably.
- Accountability — owning actions and accepting consequences.
- Clean boundaries — clear limits that protect dignity and safety.
- Courage — choosing the right action despite fear.
- Restraint — holding back harmful expression or impulse.
- Due process — fair procedure before judgment or penalty.
- Non-retaliation — refusing revenge; ending escalation.
- Stewardship of power — using authority to serve and protect.

Repair qualities (how love rebuilds):

- Ownership — admitting responsibility without excuses.
- Apology — naming harm with remorse and respect.
- Changed behavior — proving sincerity through new actions.
- Restitution — making tangible amends where possible.
- Reconciliation — rebuilding relationship where safe and desired.
- Mercy — compassion that withholds retaliation and offers repair.
- Patience — the strength to wait without resentment.
- Persistence — continuing repair efforts over time.
- Humility — willingness to learn, yield, and not self-exalt.
- Repair — restoring trust through ownership and changed behavior.

IV. One-Sentence Prompts

- "I feel ____. I want to express this with ____."
- "This matters to me. I want to speak with ____."
- "I'm feeling a lot right now. Let me slow down and choose ____."
- "I'm upset, and I want to handle this with ____."
- "I need a pause. I want to come back with ____."

445

Key reminder:

Feelings do not need permission to exist. Expression needs quality. Trust the feeling. Choose the quality. Take one small step.

V. Quality equations

A quality equation is a short equation that pairs human weather (emotion, pressure, impulse, or circumstance) with a quality or skill, producing a usable outcome. It is not a magic spell. It is an attention director.

The basic pattern is:

Weather + Quality = Outcome

In the SC series, you can treat quality equations as a practical way of asking Jesus for the next quality. They are a language for cooperation with the Holy Spirit.

VI. Quality equation Library

The lists below are organized so you can find a higher-quality next step quickly.

Where quality equations Fit in Culture

Every culture runs on compressed language: sayings, mottos, norms, and "what we do here." quality equations are QLS's version of that compression—short equations that turn abstract values into usable leadership under pressure. In modern life, the weather changes fast: group chats, classrooms, workplaces, families, meetings, and public moments can shift from calm to storm in seconds. In those moments, people don't need a lecture—they need a next step. quality equations function like road signs in fog: they don't force anyone, but they make the higher-quality path easier to see. As a leadership method, QLS uses quality equations to create a shared operating language. Instead of arguing over ego ("who's right?"), people can declare loyalty to a value system ("what quality leads next?"). Used consistently, formulas become part of a culture's reflexes: how we correct without humiliating, disagree without contempt, repair quickly, and protect dignity when the weather is harsh. A healthy culture isn't the absence of storms. It's the presence of repeatable moves—small sentences and actions—that restore direction, safety, and trust.

What a quality equation Is

A quality equation is a short equation that pairs a piece of human weather (emotion, pressure, impulse, or circumstance) with a quality or skill, producing a usable outcome. It is not a magic spell. It is an attention director.

QLS pattern:

Weather (or pressure) + Quality (or skill) = Outcome

Two guiding ideas:

1) You don't need certainty to move forward—you need a quality for the next step.

2) Under pressure, the shortest usable sentence often wins.

How to Use quality equations in the Moment

- Name the weather (one sentence, no blame).
- Call the next quality (what makes the next two minutes safer and more workable).
- Choose a formula that fits, then take one visible step (question, boundary, apology, clarification, repair).
- If you miss, repair quickly: the culture is built by the restart.

This three-step practice is the practical expression of Chapter 11's teaching on pain and joy as the two axes of consciousness.

Core QLS Formulas

Possible + Quality = Desirable

Fear + Courage = Intervention

Power + Restraint = Protection

Alarm + Leadership = Order

Anger + Fairness = Justice

Correction + Respect = Coaching

Authority + Humility = Leadership

Mistake + Ownership = Trust

Apology + Changed Behavior = Repair

Boundary + Respect = Safety

Anger + Restraint = Containment

Fear + Courage = Leadership

Anger + Restraint = Protection

Hurt + Honesty = Repair

Uncertainty + Quality = Direction

Instability + Repair = Stability

Pain + Objection = Fixation (Trauma Loop)

Pain + Acceptance + Quality = Integration

Pain + Faith + Quality = Return Toward Joy

Directional Formulas

Unchosen Quality → Worry

Chosen Quality → Readiness

Values Without Skills → Collapse Under Pressure

Chosen Quality + First Sentence → Confidence

Anger Formulas

Anger is weather—energy that often signals a boundary, a value, or a harm. Pair it with quality to produce clean power.

Anger + Pause = Choice

Anger + Breath = Steadiness

Anger + Restraint = Containment

Anger + Slowness = Precision

Anger + Grounding = Stability

Anger + Time = Clarity

Anger + Space = Safety

Anger + Silence = Self-control

Anger + Patience = Endurance

Anger + Discipline = Direction

Anger + Plan = Confidence

Anger + Structure = Order

Anger + Routine = Regulation

Anger + Self-care = Recovery

Anger + Sleep = Perspective

Anger + Hydration = Regulation

Anger + Acceptance = Mobility

Anger + Humility = Groundedness

Anger + Respect = Dignity

Anger + Civility = Influence

Anger + Curiosity = Inquiry

Anger + Listening = Understanding

Anger + Empathy = Compassion

Anger + Kindness = Gentleness

Anger + Tact = Diplomacy

Anger + Clarity = Clean Request

Anger + Directness = Candor

Anger + Truthfulness = Honesty

Anger + Transparency = Trust

Anger + Consent = Respectful Contact

Anger + Permission = Agency

Anger + Questions = Dialogue

Anger + Neutral Tone = Usable Message

Anger + I-statements = Clean Confrontation

Anger + Courage = Boundary

Anger + Firmness = Safety

Anger + Limits = Protection

Anger + Nonviolence = Moral Authority

Anger + Calm = Authority

Anger + Authority = Enforcement (Clean)

Anger + Responsibility = Leadership

Anger + Stewardship = Guardianship

Anger + Service = Protection

Anger + Prudence = Right Timing

Anger + Strategy = Leverage

Anger + Wisdom = Discernment

Anger + Proportion = Fair Response

Anger + Restraint = Protection

Anger + Boundary Language = Safety

Anger + Exit = De-escalation

Anger + Fairness = Justice

Anger + Evidence = Accuracy

Anger + Due Process = Legitimacy

Anger + Consistency = Credibility

Anger + Accountability = Change

Anger + Standards = Integrity

Anger + Courage = Advocacy

Anger + Patience = Persistence

Anger + Community = Reform

Anger + Policy = Protection at Scale

Anger + Restraint = Clean Justice

Anger + Respect = Just Correction

Anger + Clarity = Clean Boundary

Anger + Repair = Restoration

Anger + Forgiveness = Mercy

Anger + Grace = Mercy

Anger + Compassion = Understanding

Anger + Ownership = Trust

Anger + Accountability = Repair

Anger + Apology = Reconciliation

Anger + Repair = Renewal

Anger + Humility = Re-entry

Anger + Truthfulness = Clean Restart

Anger + Respect = Non-humiliating Correction

Anger + Patience = Second Chance

Anger + Generosity = Grace

Anger + Gentleness = Healing

Anger + Boundaries = Stable Peace

Anger + Love = Protection

Anger + Curiosity = Coaching

Anger + Correction + Respect = Coaching

Anger + Consistency = Fair Discipline

Anger + Warmth = Secure Limit

Anger + Protection = Safety Culture

Anger + Patience = Teaching

Anger + Humor = Defusion (Use Carefully)

Anger + Repair = Family Stability

Anger + Respect = Dignity-preserving Limit

Anger + Steadiness = Containment

Fear Formulas

Fear is immediate weather. Pairing fear with quality converts alarm into usable protection and motion.

Fear + Breath = Calm

Fear + Slowness = Control

Fear + Grounding = Stability

Fear + Pause = Choice

Fear + Stillness = Clarity

Fear + Time = Perspective

Fear + Body Awareness = Regulation

Fear + Hydration = Regulation

Fear + Sleep = Perspective

Fear + Warmth = Safety

Fear + Routine = Stability

Fear + Structure = Order

Fear + Self-care = Recovery

Fear + Acceptance = Mobility

Fear + Self-compassion = Recovery

Fear + Patience = Endurance

Fear + Facts = Orientation

Fear + Reality-check = Accuracy

Fear + Curiosity = Information

Fear + Questions = Data

Fear + Humility = Learning

Fear + Context = Perspective

Fear + Naming the Weather = Clarity

Fear + Truthfulness = Stability

Fear + Simplicity = Focus

Fear + One Next Step = Motion

Fear + Plan = Confidence

Fear + Preparation = Readiness

Fear + Practice = Competence

Fear + Rehearsal = Confidence

Fear + Feedback = Improvement

Fear + Courage = Action

Fear + Courage = Intervention

Fear + Courage = Leadership

Fear + Bravery = Forward Motion

Fear + Commitment = Follow-through

Fear + Consistency = Trustworthiness

Fear + Discipline = Direction

Fear + Values = Integrity

Fear + Quality = Direction

Fear + Steadiness = Authority

Fear + Restraint = Clean Action

Fear + Protective Courage = Safety

Fear + Boundaries = Safety

Fear + Limits = Protection

Fear + Exit = De-escalation

Fear + Distance = Safety

Fear + Delegation = Protection

Fear + Help-seeking = Safety

Fear + Accountability = Protection

Fear + Planning = Risk Management

Fear + Nonviolence = Moral Authority

Fear + Restraint = Containment

Fear + Clear 'No' = Boundary

Fear + Policy = Safety at Scale

Fear + Honesty = Trust

Fear + Respect = Dignity

Fear + Gentleness = Safety

Fear + Vulnerability = Connection

Fear + Ask Permission = Agency

Fear + Listening = Understanding

Fear + Empathy = Connection

Fear + Repair = Resilience

Fear + Humility = Re-entry

Fear + Apology = Repair

Fear + Clarity = Clean Request

Fear + Directness = Candor

Fear + Truth + Kindness = Usable Honesty

Fear + Preparation = Confidence

Fear + Coaching = Improvement

Fear + Feedback-seeking = Growth

Fear + Structure = Execution

Fear + Checklist = Reliability

Fear + Pacing = Endurance

Fear + Focus = Performance

Fear + Reframe = Confidence

Fear + Small Start = Momentum

Fear + One Sentence = Re-entry

Fear + Quality = Self-respect

Fear + Restraint = Protection

Fear + Delegation = Wise Protection

Fear + Teamwork = Safety

Fear + Calling an Adult = Protection

Fear + Distraction = Rescue

Fear + Dignity = Leadership

Fear + Refusal to Laugh = Integrity

Fear + Escort = Protection

Fear + Boundary = Order

Anxiety Formulas

Anxiety is forecast weather. A plan, a quality, and a first sentence often reduce the scan for danger.

Anxiety + Plan = Readiness

Anxiety + Plan = Calm

Anxiety + Sequence = Control

Anxiety + Checklist = Reliability

Anxiety + Timebox = Manageability

Anxiety + Calendar = Order

Anxiety + Preparation = Confidence

Anxiety + Rehearsal = Competence

Anxiety + First Step = Motion

Anxiety + Next Sentence = Agency

Anxiety + Practice = Capability

Anxiety + Support = Stability

Anxiety + Delegation = Relief

Anxiety + Structure = Predictability

Anxiety + Routine = Regulation

Anxiety + Breath = Steadiness

Anxiety + Grounding = Presence

Anxiety + Body Scan = Regulation

Anxiety + Movement = Discharge

Anxiety + Sleep = Perspective

Anxiety + Nutrition = Stability

Anxiety + Hydration = Regulation

Anxiety + Warmth = Safety

Anxiety + Slow Pace = Clarity

Anxiety + Silence = Calm

Anxiety + Nature = Settling

Anxiety + Meditation = Centering

Anxiety + Facts = Orientation

Anxiety + Reality-check = Accuracy

Anxiety + Probability = Perspective

Anxiety + Naming the Fear = Clarity

Anxiety + Curiosity = Information

Anxiety + Questions = Data

Anxiety + Write it Down = Containment

Anxiety + Sorting = Clarity

Anxiety + Priorities = Direction

Anxiety + One Task = Focus

Anxiety + Acceptance = Mobility

Anxiety + Quality = Direction

Anxiety + Meaning = Integration

Anxiety + Chosen Quality = Readiness

Anxiety + Chosen Quality = Calm

Anxiety + Quality + First Sentence = Confidence

Anxiety + Rehearsed Quality = Stability

Anxiety + Quality Commitment = Self-trust

Anxiety + Plan for Repair = Fear Reduction

Anxiety + Permission to Restart = Safety

Anxiety + If-Then Plan = Confidence

Anxiety + Exit Plan = Safety

Anxiety + Help Plan = Relief

Anxiety + Ask Permission = Safety

Anxiety + Respect = Dignity

Anxiety + Honesty = Trust

Anxiety + Clarity = Clean Request

Anxiety + Boundaries = Safety

Anxiety + Repair = Resilience

Anxiety + Listening = Understanding

Anxiety + Empathy = Connection

Anxiety + Truth + Kindness = Usable Honesty

Anxiety + Patience = Endurance

Anxiety + Humility = Re-entry

Anxiety + Orientation = Now

Anxiety + Ground = Safety

Anxiety + Restraint = Containment

Anxiety + Self-care = Recovery

Anxiety + Truthfulness = Stability

Anxiety + One Safe Person = Support

Anxiety + Repair = Integration

Anxiety + Plan = Stability

Anxiety + Protection = Safety

Other QLS Formula Libraries

Locomotion, Quality, and Identity

Pressure + Plan = Calm

Pressure + Quality = Direction

Emotion + Quality = Usable Energy

Impulse + Pause = Choice

Choice + Follow-through = Integrity

Quality + Repetition = Character

Character + Consistency = Reputation

Reputation + Trust = Influence

Influence + Humility = Leadership

Shame, Mistakes, and Self-Repair

Shame + Secrecy = Stuckness

Shame + Compassion = Repair

Shame + Truthfulness = Freedom

Shame + Safe Disclosure = Relief

Embarrassment + Humor = Lightness

Embarrassment + Courage = Re-entry

Embarrassment + Respect = Dignity

Self-attack + Truth = Damage

Self-honesty + Kindness = Growth

Failure + Coaching = Improvement

Failure + Meaning = Maturity

Guilt, Regret, and Accountability

Guilt + Ownership = Repair

Guilt + Action = Restoration

Guilt + Shame = Collapse

Regret + Plan = Growth

Regret + Courage = Apology

Regret + Repair = Renewal

Responsibility + Follow-through = Reliability

Accountability + Dignity = Safety

Accountability + Contempt = Revolt

Truth + Accountability = Trust

Grief, Sadness, and Integration

Sadness + Acceptance = Softening

Sadness + Meaning = Integration

Grief + Time = Healing

Grief + Support = Endurance

Grief + Ritual = Integration

Loss + Love = Honor

Pain + Presence = Healing

Pain + Meaning = Integration

Pain + Quality = Forward Motion

Suffering + Isolation = Despair

Suffering + Connection = Endurance

Envy, Comparison, and Insecurity

Envy + Admiration = Inspiration

Envy + Curiosity = Learning

Envy + Discipline = Progress

Jealousy + Honesty = Clarity

Jealousy + Boundaries = Safety

Comparison + Gratitude = Contentment

Comparison + Plan = Progress

Insecurity + Quality = Self-respect

Insecurity + Performance = Exhaustion

Insecurity + Truth = Stability

Desire, Temptation, and Discipline

Desire + Discipline = Progress

Desire + Patience = Maturity

Temptation + Restraint = Freedom

Temptation + Secrecy = Addiction

Craving + Delay = Control

Impulse + Environment Design = Success

Urgency + Calm = Effectiveness

Urgency + Speed = Mistakes

Urgency + Priorities = Focus

Urgency + Sequence = Execution

Stress, Overload, and Sustainability

Stress + Boundaries = Sustainability
Stress + Priorities = Focus
Stress + Delegation = Relief
Overload + Sorting = Clarity
Overload + One Next Step = Motion
Fatigue + Rest = Recovery
Fatigue + Discipline = Burnout
Burnout + Self-care = Return
Chaos + Structure = Order
Noise + Silence = Clarity

Conflict, Authority, and Clean Power

Conflict + Respect = Dialogue
Conflict + Curiosity = Understanding
Conflict + Clarity = Boundary
Conflict + Contempt = War
Disagreement + Listening = Learning
Disagreement + Humility = Progress
Boundary + Love = Protection
Power + Humility = Authority
Authority + Fairness = Legitimacy
Authority + Humiliation = Rebellion
Correction + Contempt = Damage
Strength + Gentleness = Safety
Firmness + Warmth = Secure Limit

Repair Culture

Rupture + Repair = Resilience

Truth + Repair = Trust

Repair + Speed = Stability

Repair + Specificity = Credibility

Repair + Repetition = Culture

Repair + Public Dignity = Leadership

Ownership + Next Step = Reliability

Grace + Standards = Excellence

Relationships, Values, and Negotiation

Values + Agreement = Alignment

Alignment + Consistency = Trust

Trust + Candor = Intimacy

Needs + Respect = Negotiation

Needs + Ego = Conflict

Ego + Values = Humility

Values + Commitment = Loyalty

Loyalty + Boundaries = Safety

Love + Standards = Security

Conflict + Shared Values = Cooperation

We + Values = Team

Team + Repair = Longevity

Learning, Feedback, and Performance

Feedback + Curiosity = Growth

Feedback + Shame = Shutdown

Feedback + Plan = Improvement

Criticism + Humility = Learning

Criticism + Pride = War

Practice + Quality = Mastery

Practice + Consistency = Skill

Talent + Discipline = Excellence

Discipline + Joy = Sustainability

Coaching + Respect = Development

Pressure + Rehearsal = Confidence

Trauma and Recovery

Alarm + Plan = Calm

Trigger + Grounding = Presence

Shock + Orientation = Now

Pain + Acceptance = Mobility

Acceptance + Quality = Integration

Memory + Meaning = Integration

Survival + Support = Recovery

Protection + Re-entry = Healing

Story + Quality = Identity Repair

Anti-Formulas (Warning Pairings)

These pairings often feel protective in the moment but reliably create damage. Treat them as "storm warnings."

Anger + Contempt = Cruelty

Anger + Humiliation = Revenge

Anger + Sarcasm = Damage

Anger + Certainty = Tyranny

Anger + Speed = Regret

Anger + Mind-reading = False Accusation

Anger + Alcohol = Chaos

Anger + Dogpile = Mob Harm

Fear + Avoidance = Shrinking Life

Fear + Aggression = Regret

Fear + Control = Rigidity

Fear + Contempt = Cruelty

Fear + Blame = Conflict

Fear + Speed = Mistake

Fear + Silence (Withholding) = Distance

Anxiety + Catastrophizing = Panic

Anxiety + Rumination = Stuckness

Anxiety + Reassurance Addiction = Dependence

Anxiety + Control = Exhaustion

Anxiety + Overchecking = More Anxiety

Anxiety + Avoidance = Phobia Loop

Anxiety + Shame = Collapse

Ladders (Quick Sets)

Ladders are short sequences of formulas that describe a stepwise improvement in quality.

Anger Ladder

Anger + Restraint = Containment

Anger + Clarity = Boundary

Anger + Fairness = Justice

Anger + Forgiveness = Mercy

Fear Ladder

Fear + Breath = Calm

Fear + Facts = Orientation

Fear + Quality = Direction

Fear + Courage = Action

Anxiety Ladder

Anxiety + Grounding = Presence

Anxiety + Plan = Readiness

Anxiety + Quality = Direction

Anxiety + First Step = Motion

Repair Ladder

Mistake + Ownership = Trust

Truth + Repair = Trust

Apology + Changed Behavior = Repair

Rupture + Repair = Resilience

Conflict Ladder

Conflict + Respect = Dialogue

Conflict + Clarity = Boundary

Conflict + Fairness = Justice

Conflict + Repair = Resilience

Authority Ladder

> Power + Restraint = Protection
> Power + Humility = Authority
> Authority + Fairness = Legitimacy
> Authority + Humility = Leadership

Formula Generator (How to Coin New Ones)

Use these templates to generate new formulas that match your voice and context:

> Weather + Quality = Outcome
> Pressure + Skill = Stability
> Rupture + Repair = Resilience
> Boundary + Respect = Safety
> Truth + Kindness = Usable Honesty

A practical test: if you can say the formula in a hard moment and it helps you choose a better next sentence, it belongs in QLS.

VII. Expanded Anger Library

Anger is energy. It can become damage, or it can become protection, justice, repair, and clean boundary. The difference is the quality you add.

> Anger + Clarity = Clean request
> Anger + Consent = Respectful contact

Anger + Neutral tone = Usable message

Anger + "I-statements" = Clean confrontation

Anger + Nonviolence = Moral authority

Anger + Authority = Enforcement (clean)

Anger + Prudence = Right timing

Anger + Proportion = Fair response

Anger + Boundary language = Safety

Anger + Due process = Legitimacy

Anger + Policy = Protection at scale

Anger + Restraint = Clean justice

Anger + Respect = Just correction

Anger + Clarity = Clean boundary

Anger + Forgiveness = Mercy

Anger + Truthfulness = Clean restart

Anger + Respect = Non-humiliating correction

Anger + Patience = Second chance

Anger + Boundaries = Stable peace

Anger + Correction + Respect = Coaching (a classic QLS pairing)

Anger + Consistency = Fair discipline

Anger + Warmth = Secure limit

Anger + Protection = Safety culture

Anger + Humor = Defusion (use carefully—never at someone's dignity)

Anger + Repair = Family stability

Anger + Respect = Dignity-preserving limit

Anger + Mind-reading = False accusation

Anger + Dogpile = Mob harm

Fear + Body awareness = Regulation
Fear + Naming the weather = Clarity
Fear + One next step = Motion
Fear + Bravery = Forward motion
Fear + Restraint = Clean action
Fear + Protective courage = Safety
Fear + Planning = Risk management
Fear + Nonviolence = Moral authority
Fear + Clear "No" = Boundary
Fear + Policy = Safety at scale
Fear + Ask permission = Agency
Fear + Clarity = Clean request
Fear + Truth + kindness = Usable honesty
Fear + Small start = Momentum
Fear + One sentence = Re-entry
Fear + Delegation = Wise protection
Fear + Calling an adult = Protection
Fear + Refusal to laugh = Integrity
Anxiety + First step = Motion
Anxiety + Next sentence = Agency
Anxiety + Body scan = Regulation
Anxiety + Slow pace = Clarity
Anxiety + Prayer/meditation = Centering
Anxiety + Naming the fear = Clarity
Anxiety + Write it down = Containment
Anxiety + One task = Focus
Anxiety + Chosen quality = Readiness
Anxiety + Chosen quality = Calm

Anxiety + Quality + first sentence = Confidence

Anxiety + Rehearsed quality = Stability

Anxiety + Quality commitment = Self-trust

Anxiety + Plan for repair = Fear reduction

Anxiety + Permission to restart = Safety

Anxiety + "If-then" plan = Confidence

Anxiety + Exit plan = Safety

Anxiety + Help plan = Relief

Anxiety + Ask permission = Safety

Anxiety + Clarity = Clean request

Anxiety + Truth + kindness = Usable honesty

Anxiety + One safe person = Support

Fear + Avoidance = Shrinking life

Fear + Silence (withholding) = Distance

Anxiety + Reassurance addiction = Dependence

Anxiety + Overchecking = More anxiety

Anxiety + Avoidance = Phobia loop

Anxiety + First step = Motion

Final reminder: Feelings are weather. Qualities are steering. You do not have to become less human to become more holy; you only have to choose what love does next.

Appendix B

A Prayer for the Disturbed Soul

"Jesus, this hurts, and I acknowledge that it hurts. Pain is not the whole truth. Light still exists. Joy still exists. I want to cope with pain well so that I can join the joy of Heaven. I want to love You, and I do not know how. Please show me. Protect my desire. Keep me from reacting only from pain. Give me the next quality. Teach me to honor pain, rejoice in existence, practice love, and return again and again to the joy for which You made me."

In this way, faith, pain, prayer, and qualities are not separate subjects. They are one movement of consciousness under Jesus: the soul is hurt, the soul tells the truth, the soul believes that joy still exists, the soul asks for the next quality, and the soul keeps walking until the weather no longer decides what it becomes.

Appendix C – Formula Assemblies for the Four Levels of Religion

This appendix gathers the developmental formulas introduced in Chapter 20A. Its purpose is practical: to help the reader, teacher, pastor, parent, or counselor translate one spiritual situation through the four levels of religion—rules, reasons for rules, apprehension of qualities, and awareness of Jesus. The appendix is especially concerned with the key developmental insight that souls in the earlier stages usually need help seeing, naming, and appreciating qualities before those qualities can become stable in character.

I. Why Levels One and Two Need Help Seeing Qualities

Stage One and Stage Two are not yet stages of spiritual beauty. They are stages of protection and understanding. At Stage One the soul asks, "What must I do?" At Stage Two it asks, "Why is this good?" Only at Stage Three does the soul begin to ask, "What quality is shining here?" The movement into qualities therefore requires assistance. The soul must be helped to notice fruit, to admire what produced it, and to recognize that the admired quality is something a soul can begin to want for itself.

For this reason, qualities must often be made visible before they can be loved. Earlier-stage souls usually see examples before abstractions, consequences before beauty, and concrete goodness before inward form. The teacher must therefore point from action to fruit, from fruit to quality, and from quality to Jesus.

II. Bridge Formulas That Move the Soul Toward Qualities

The bridge may be stated in extended form:

  rule + concrete example = visible quality

  rule + repetition = habit

  habit + noticed fruit = respect for the rule

  reason + reflection on the fruit = recognition of the quality

  recognized quality + admiration = appreciation of the quality

  appreciated quality + practice = beginning virtue

472

virtue + awareness of Jesus = communion

A shorter bridge says the same thing:

command + action = obedience

obedience + good fruit = meaning

meaning + named quality = appreciation

appreciation + Jesus = discipleship

The four stages themselves can be summarized this way:

Stage One: struggle + commanded practice = guarded life

Stage Two: struggle + understood good = wise life

Stage Three: struggle + quality = formed character

Stage Four: struggle + Jesus' presence = communion and fruit

III. Formula Assemblies by Quality

Faith

Stage One: anxiety + pray before reacting = steadier behavior

Stage Two: steadier behavior + noticing God's care = appreciation of faith

Stage Three: anxiety + faith = stability

Stage Four: anxiety + awareness of Jesus' presence = peace

Humility

Stage One: correction + no self-defense = teachable response

Stage Two: teachable response + seeing growth = appreciation of humility

Stage Three: weakness + humility = growth

Stage Four: humility + following Jesus = likeness to Christ

Patience

Stage One: delay + no grumbling = restrained response

Stage Two: restrained response + seeing good timing = appreciation of patience

Stage Three: waiting + patience = endurance

Stage Four: waiting + trust in Jesus = restful hope

Mercy

Stage One: offense + no retaliation = restrained harm

Stage Two: restrained harm + preserved relationship = appreciation of mercy

Stage Three: offense + mercy = forgiveness

Stage Four: offense + awareness of Jesus' mercy = reconciliation

Truthfulness

Stage One: pressure + tell the truth = honest speech

Stage Two: honest speech + growing trust = appreciation of integrity

Stage Three: speech + truthfulness = integrity

Stage Four: speech + abiding in Jesus the Truth = freedom

Generosity

Stage One: possessions + giving rule = practiced sharing

Stage Two: practiced sharing + seeing another helped = appreciation of generosity

Stage Three: possessions + generosity = stewardship

Stage Four: possessions + awareness of Jesus' self-giving = cheerful charity

Purity

Stage One: desire + boundary = protected action

Stage Two: protected action + seeing love safeguarded = appreciation of purity

Stage Three: desire + chastity = integrated love

Stage Four: desire + abiding in Jesus = holy desire

Hope

Stage One: suffering + remain faithful = persevering action

Stage Two: persevering action + discovering meaning = appreciation of hope

Stage Three: suffering + hope = resilience

Stage Four: suffering + union with Jesus = redemptive endurance

Compassion

Stage One: neighbor's need + serve = concrete care

Stage Two: concrete care + seeing another strengthened = appreciation of compassion

Stage Three: need + compassion = love in action

Stage Four: need + seeing Jesus in the other = charity

Gratitude

Stage One: blessing received + give thanks = remembered gift

Stage Two: remembered gift + less entitlement = appreciation of gratitude

Stage Three: abundance or lack + gratitude = contentment

Stage Four: life + awareness of Jesus as gift = worship

IV. Teaching Questions That Help Earlier-Stage Souls Notice Qualities

The following questions help a Stage One or Stage Two soul move toward Stage Three without contempt or confusion:

What pain was this rule trying to prevent?

What good fruit appeared when the rule was kept?

What quality was shining in that fruit?

What becomes safer, stronger, or more beautiful when that quality is lived?

Where do I see Jesus embodying this quality?

What is one visible next action by which I can practice it?

The aim is not to skip the earlier stages, but to interpret them so fully that they open into qualities and finally into Christ-awareness. When this happens, rules are no longer felt as mere restraint and reasons are no longer felt as mere explanation. Both become pathways by which the soul learns to love the good.

Possible + Quality = Desirable
QUALITY LEADERSHIP SYSTEMS
Quality Directs.
Mind guides.
Emotion energizes.
Body acts.
QLS
Truth + Kindness = Candor • Mistake + Repair = Trust